W9-ABC-025

a sisterchicks® devotional

SISTERCHICKS IN THE WORD:

TAKE FLIGHT!

ROBIN JONES GUNN
AND CINDY HANNAN

Multnomah ® Publishers *Sisters, Oregon*

TAKE FLIGHT!

published by Multnomah Publishers, Inc.

© 2006 by Robin's Ink, LLC

International Standard Book Number: 1-59052-537-X

Sisterchicks is a trademark of Multnomah Publishers, Inc.

Cover image by Herrman/Starke/Corbis

Unless otherwise indicated, Scripture quotations are from:

The Message by Eugene H. Peterson

© 1993, 1994, 1995, 1996, 2000, 2001, 2002

Used by permission of Navpress Publishing Group

All rights reserved.

Other Scripture quotations are from:

The Holy Bible, New International Version (NIV) © 1973, 1984 by International Bible Society.

Used by permission of Zondervan Publishing House

Holy Bible, New Living Translation (NLT) © 1996.

Used by permission of Tyndale Charitable Trust. All rights reserved.

The Living Bible (TLB) © 1971.

Used by permission of Tyndale House Publishers, Inc. All rights reserved.

"I'll Fly Away" by Albert E. Brumley

© 1932 in "Wonderful Message" by Hartford Music Co. Renewed 1960 by Albert E. Brumley
& Sons/SESAC (admin. By ICG). All rights reserved. Used by permission.

Interior design by Robin Black, Blackbird Creative, Bend, OR.

Multnomah is a trademark of Multnomah Publishers, Inc., and is registered
in the U.S. Patent and Trademark Office.

The colophon is a trademark of Multnomah Publishers, Inc.

Printed in the United States of America

LIBRARY OF CONGRESS CATALOGING-IN-PUBLICATION DATA

Gunn, Robin Jones, 1955-
  Take flight! : a Sisterchicks devotional / Robin Jones Gunn and Cindy Hannan.
    p. cm.
  ISBN 1-59052-537-X
  1. Christian women—Religious life. I. Hannan, Cindy. II. Title.
BV4527.G87 2006
242'.643—dc22

2006020276

For information:
MULTNOMAH PUBLISHERS, INC.
601 N. Larch Street
SISTERS, OREGON 97759

06 07 08 09 10 11—10 9 8 7 6 5 4 3 2 1 0

"Do this and live," the law commands
But gives me neither feet nor hands.
A better thing this grace now brings
It bids me fly and gives me wings!

—ADAPTED FROM A QUOTE ATTRIBUTED TO
JOHN BUNYAN ENTITLED "RUN, JOHN, RUN"

Contents

*A*h, grace. Grace that would bid us fly and give us wings! What a welcoming image—being set free to become all God intended and to soar through life.

Why is it, then, that such freedom often feels like an elusive dream? We hold back. We hesitate. He lifts the cage's latch and invites us to take flight. We step to the edge and...

Sometimes we soar. Sometimes we tumble. Yet here's a secret: Every soar, every tumble, every frantic flapping about, is covered by God's grace, His grace upon grace. Every escapade with Him becomes a story.

In *Take Flight!* we want to explore those stories—the grace-stories of life. Whether you flit through these pages alone or with a fine feathered Sisterchick or two, we think you'll see your own grace-stories between the lines. You'll be reminded that even in moments that seemed graceless, God's hand kept you from tumbling into oblivion. And His grace will keep you from future free falls regardless of what awaits you.

I'd like to start off by telling you a grace-story about my friend Cindy and how the two of us came to write this book. For more than a decade, Cindy and I have met with our friend Carrie every Tuesday morning to pray. This journey has knit our hearts together in rich and abiding ways.

About the time I was considering writing a devotional book, Cindy returned from a trip to Indonesia where she had met with a group of women involved in mission work. Cindy's time with the women included interacting around a series of discussion questions and reflections on Scripture that she had prepared ahead of time. The women opened their hearts to each other, and the results were sweetly eternal.

Cindy told me about her Indonesian experience while we were driving to Central Oregon. I slowed the car and pulled into an empty campsite under a canopy of ancient towering evergreens.

"Cindy, we could do this together!"

"Do what?"

"We could write a devotional book together. A nouveau devo! You could do what you do so well—ask gentle questions. And I'll do what I do—tell God-stories. What do you think?"

Neither of us knew quite what to think, but we exited the car, stood with our arms and faces raised toward the heavens, and sang. It was pretty amazing, especially for a couple of conservative Sisterchicks like us. I don't even remember what we sang. What I do remember is that something in our spirits took flight that August morning in the moss-scented forest. We were willing to take a risk. Try something new. Trust God in a new way.

In the months following our collective chirp of a "yes" to the Lord, the format took shape. I would use a quote from a character in a Sisterchicks novel as a launching pad to tell a real-life story of grace, dubbing the tale "From Robin's Nest." Cindy would take to her perch with her laptop and write questions based on the story, adding flourishes of wisdom, wit, and whimsy.

With our plan settled on, we hunkered down and did what all writers do. We wrote—and rewrote and rewrote.

Now, from our kindred spirits, Cindy and I present to you this nouveau devo with a few Sisterchicky flourishes. And don't worry one flutter if you've never heard of a "Sisterchick" until this moment. By definition, a *Sisterchick* is "a friend who shares the deepest wonders of your heart, loves you like a sister, and gives you a reality check when you're being a brat." Whether you meet regularly with a gaggle of Sisterchicks or don't have a Sisterchick in your life at the moment, this book is for you. If you've read every Sisterchicks novel or never peered at a single one, you belong right here. We are oh so eager for you to dive into the birdbath with us.

May the words we've lined up in this book spark in you and your Sisterchicks a deeper love for our heavenly Father and for His unending grace. He has lifted the latch on your cage. Come closer to Him. No, closer. Lean over the edge of endless freedom and possibilities, and see what happens when your spirit takes flight.

All atwitter,

Robin

"God's Spirit beckons. There are things to do and places to go!" (Romans 8:14)

Bird's—Eye View

"From heaven the LORD looks down
and sees all mankind;
from his dwelling place he watches
all who live on earth—
he who forms the hearts of all,
who considers everything they do."

PSALM 33:13–15, NIV

"To look at everything always as though
you were seeing it either for the first or last time:
Thus is your time on earth filled with glory."

BETTY SMITH, A TREE GROWS IN BROOKLYN

Sunset Worship

"I want to live each day with a full, open heart
to the Lord and always be thankful for what He does.
Now, exactly how do I do that?"

—SHARON, *SISTERCHICKS ON THE LOOSE!*

Last summer my husband and I hosted a small party for a few friends. We gathered in the backyard, where we ate, talked, and laughed. As evening approached, the sky changed colors. A cloud blanket spun of rich pink satin hues came rolling over the violet sky. Conversations stopped. Everyone looked up.

Spontaneously, we moved to the front yard for an unobstructed view. We stood like a grove of humans planted in a row. Together we watched the colors deepen as the sun slowly withdrew its illuminating light. It was the most extraordinary sunset ever.

A soft breeze wearing velvet slippers sashayed through the birch trees. With a ripple of unashamed delight, the trees clapped their hands.

We were receiving a gift, and I knew it. This was a glimpse of God's glory. It was as if His royal robes were brushing the canopy of earth's atmosphere as He passed by. From the forest of evergreens at the end of our street, a flock of birds rose. They soared like dark polka dots on an invisible kite, rising into the elevated pinkness of the twilight. As we listened, the birds cried out their praises, too.

Deep inside me was a whisper, an inclination to kneel, to bow face-first. Not to worship creation, but the Creator of this magnificent display of glory.

However, I am a proud creature. Other planted humans were watching me. Unlike the birds and the trees, I didn't release the praise welling up inside. Instead, I stood unmoving and leaked a few oohs and aahs as the sun took a final dip behind the west Portland hills. All around us the subdued shades of night closed in.

On many nights since, when nothing but darkness and dull, gray rain clouds shroud the sky, I've wondered what it would have been like to openly offer a sacrifice of praise on that dazzling summer night. What would have happened if the birds hadn't so spontaneously exalted in the moment? What if the trees hadn't celebrated with every one of their leaves? Would the rocks have cried out?

My daughter, Rachel, isn't so proud that she conceals her expressions of praise. When she was five, we lived in Hawaii, and our family often took evening walks along the beach. Rachel would dance along the shoreline and sing out,

WIT 'N' WHIMSY

"Worship is all that I am, responding to all that God is through Jesus Christ."

–MATT HANNAN

"Come, crinkle, curl, splash!" She used her arms to orchestrate the waves and then twirled around as she repeated her song over and over.

One night I asked what her words meant. She looked surprised. "Don't you hear it, Mom? It's in the wind. God's telling the ocean what to do, and the ocean is obeying."

Come

Crinkle

Curl

Splash

Her freshman year of college, Rachel went to a Southern California university. The first week in the dorm a group of women from her floor shuttled to Newport Beach to soak up the sun. Rachel went for a walk alone along the shore, so happy in her young heart to be beside the ocean.

The waves had left what she referred to as "shell crumbs" along the shore in a long, wavy trail. Reaching for a handful, Rachel nestled in the warm sand and used her fingers to sift through all the broken pieces. One small, white, rounded shell stuck to the tip of her index finger and stayed there, perfectly fitting like a tiny cap. At the top of the shell was a miniscule pinhole.

When Rachel came home on a break, she was wearing the single shell around her wrist on a bracelet she had made.

"Mom, did I tell you about this shell yet?" Her tone made it clear she was sharing a special secret. "I had asked God for a word that would represent my spiritual journey this semester. As I was walking on the beach, I looked out at the ocean and remembered living in Hawaii. Then I heard the calming command I used to hear God giving to the waves. But you know what, Mom? This time it was different."

I leaned in, eager to hear what Rachel would say.

"There was a new line at the end of the command. What surprised me was that the new line fit so perfectly."

"What was it?"

"Come

    Crinkle

       Curl

          Splash

             ...Listen to Me."

"That was it? 'Listen to Me'?" I don't know what I had expected, but as I considered the phrase, it did seem like a good fit.

"Yeah. You can hear the whole ocean in even the smallest shell if you're quiet enough and listen. That's what the Lord was asking me to do. To listen to Him. Every time I see this tiny shell on my bracelet, I remember."

Three months later, my husband and I were back in Hawaii. The two of us had spent the afternoon swimming and sunning on our favorite beach when sunset hushed over us. I heard that distinctive whisper in my spirit beckoning me to offer up a sacrifice of praise. *Come, crinkle, curl, splash... listen to Me.*

This time I didn't hold back. It was my turn to listen and obey. I went back into the water, arms raised, singing as loud as I could. With my face toward the sunset, I danced my heart out before Creator God in the most bumbling demonstration of interpretive water ballet ever. But I think He liked it.

At least the rocks got to hold their tongue one more night.

*W*hen we listen carefully, we find that God calls us to divine appointments at the most surprising times: sunrise, sunset, alone, in a crowd, on a beach, in the family room.

Sometimes we come wholeheartedly, listening to God and responding to Him with abandon. Other times we look around, cough nervously, and arrive halfheartedly, hearing but not authentically responding.

God knows our hearts, and He patiently asks us to bring more of ourselves to Him than we have before. He waits for us to realize that when we worship, there is an audience of only One.

Look at how God's people responded to Him in worship in the past:

- 2 Samuel 6:14. King David did *what?*
- 2 Chronicles 6:13. King Solomon showed no stage fright here.
- Psalm 95:6. Let's all get creaky together.
- Ezekiel 43:2–4. One man's response to God's power.

What does authentic worship look like in your life? Has the way you express worship changed as your relationship with Christ has grown?

When Jesus was talking with a woman about true worship, He said, "God is sheer being itself—Spirit. Those who worship him must do it out of their very being, their spirits, their true selves, in adoration" (John 4:24).

Let's grow together in our ability to enter into unhindered worship. Ready to meet the Lover of our souls, listening with a heart willing to respond. Then let's worship as if no one is watching. Except the only One who matters.

TAKE A CLOSER LOOK

- Luke 1:46–55. Mary's song of praise.
- Psalm 27:6. Raise the roof!
- Romans 12:1. Here's what God wants us to do.

A Peep or Two from You

Christmas 2016

Lamaal comes home with a girlfriend named Crystal. First time! She is pretty and smart, a Christian and she loves my nephew. Pam and Ralph like her very much. This is good! Also, Laquel comes home, then before I got to see her, she drives with Aunt Jeanette to America's Georgia to bring back a former student of hers whose family abandoned him and he had no where to go. We gave him a great Christmas. He said he hadn't received gifts for many years. His mom left him with water, Gatorade and $20 and didn't ask or offer him a ride home to north carolina for christmas so we took him in, fed him gave him loving and great fun for Christmas. Next year Raquel goes to Dubai to work for 2½ years, coming home every 6 months. She's ready and excited. Lamaal works in hotel mgmt I think. Thank you Lord for friends and family and

Ron Barrington's still alive

related and to so with the flow better in 2017. I pray to be more Amen.

 WISDOM

QUOTABLE SISTERCHICKS

"How often, Lord, our grateful eyes
Have seen what Thou hast done,
How often does Thy love surprise
From dawn to set of sun.

Our love is like a little pool,
Thy love is like the sea,
O beautiful, O wonderful,
How noble Love can be."

AMY CARMICHAEL

 SISTERCHICKIN' SUGGESTIONS

Time to go SISTERCHICKIN'! (Slang for "Sisterchicking"—when Sisterchicks do things together, as in, "Don't bother us now. We're *SISTERCHICKIN'!*" Not to be confused with a sister-chicken.)

Field Trip Next Sunday!

Invite a friend or two to visit a church in your area that has a worship style different from your home church. Enter with an open heart, ready to celebrate not evaluate.

Love of Strangers

*"I wanted to live out the rest of my days expressing
that same extravagant love to others. I didn't want to be cautious and live
out a string of unfulfilled days, pitifully folded up
into myself. I wanted full days and a full life."*
—KATHY, *SISTERCHICKS DOWN UNDER!*

When I was in my midtwenties, I found myself the guest of a large family that ran a behind-the-scenes ministry from their home in the Austrian Alps. I had been there a few days when another guest arrived well after dark. She wasn't expected as far as I could tell. In her midteens, the young woman was shivering and spoke only Russian. Hot soup was quickly prepared for her and served in a thick wooden bowl. She sat by the fire, her thin arms lifting the steaming nourishment to her cracked lips.

Several family members understood her words as she pieced together her story. I understood nothing. One of the older boys in the family, Karl, must have read my expression because he leaned over and in English said to me, "Her name is Alenka. She has had a hard go of it. That is all you need to know. She will share your room."

I wasn't in a position to argue, but there was a slight problem. The small guest room had only one bed.

That night I fell asleep under the down comforter, listening to the steady breathing of the stranger beside me. She smelled like moss and damp earth.

Alenka didn't rise for breakfast the next morning, nor did she join the rest of us for the main family meal at noon. She slept through the day, rising in the evening and finding her way into the kitchen for a bowl of stew and a thick slice of brown bread smeared with butter. The mother of the house helped her into a warm bath and provided clean clothes since Alenka had brought nothing with her.

When I went to bed that night, Alenka entered the room with a rosy glow returning to her complexion. She carried a small glass of berry juice, which she held out to me. With animated gestures she urged me to drink the juice even though she had none for herself. I propped myself up in bed, dumbfounded at her kindness.

Alenka positioned herself cross-legged on top of our thick comforter and sat up straight. The moonlight through the window fell on her hands, folded daintily in her lap. Tilting her chin up, she sang to me. Her song was painfully beautiful, like lonely flute notes on a clear winter night.

I felt so inadequate to know how to receive her graciousness and so clumsy at trying to communicate with her. That didn't stop Alenka. She gave to me both extravagantly and sincerely. Then she placed a fresh kiss on her pink fingertips and touched it to my pillow. She said something in Russian, and I responded, "Yeah, you sleep well, too."

She did.

The next morning I went looking for Karl in the barn. I was so unsettled by this waif. Why was she doing these nice things for me? We were strangers. Foreigners. According to our governments' policies at the time, we were enemies.

"Do you know the word *hospitality*?" Karl asked.

"Yes, of course."

Karl grinned. "Do you know the meaning?"

"Sure. I mean, I think so."

"The real meaning of *hospitality* is 'love of strangers.' That is what Alenka is doing. She is loving you—a stranger."

Me? A stranger? I'm an invited guest. She's the stranger!

Years later, when I had folded back into my comfortable circle of American friends, I was helping to set up for a nice dinner one night. One of the women was distraught over the table setting. The china plates didn't match. The tablecloth had a coffee stain that hadn't come out in the wash. The centerpiece was wilting, and the hostess was on the edge of tears.

"It will all turn out fine," I said, trying to cheer her up.

"I know. It's just so hard to show true hospitality without the right supplies, you know?"

I nodded sympathetically, but inwardly I was pulled back to the Austrian Alps. I saw the soft glow on Alenka's fresh-scrubbed face when she handed me the small glass of berry juice. The only supplies she had were her two willing hands and a song in the night. And that was all she needed to show extravagant love to me, a stranger.

ow beautiful and yet humbling to be the recipient of authentic hospitality.

Alenka openly gave such hospitality in the midst of her material poverty. Her expression of love to a stranger wasn't dependent on lace, china, or silver to make it lovely. Hospitality offered from the heart sparkles in any setting.

Think of a time when you felt the real deal—a heart that welcomed you with genuine love. If there was a lack of material props, did it make a difference in how you felt?

The core of the word *hospitality* is "hospital," a place of care and healing. Are our hearts and homes places where healing occurs for family, friends, and strangers the Lord brings onto our paths? When have you experienced healing because of someone's hospitality?

When we struggle with expressing authentic hospitality, we aren't alone. Have you ever heard the saying "Both fish and visitors stink after three days"? This proverb appears in various forms in cultures around the world. Nearly two thousand years ago, Peter tells first-century believers to "above all, love each other deeply, because love covers over a multitude of sins. Offer hospitality to one another without grumbling" (1 Peter 4:8–9, NIV).

What needs to be different in our hearts that would enable us to show grumbling the door and to welcome guests in?

These ancient words offer hope for the hospitality-impaired:

"Each one should use whatever gift he has received to serve others, faithfully administering God's grace in its various forms. If anyone speaks, he should do it as one speaking the very words of God. If anyone serves, he should do it with the strength God provides, so that in all things God may be praised through Jesus Christ." (1 Peter 4:10–11, NIV)

Is there someone in your world who needs your hospitality? What has God given to you that you can pass on with a good dose of love? What has God placed in your hand? Just offer it along with love and a great big smile.

Take a Closer Look

- Romans 12:13. Quick and to the point.
- Romans 16:5. What meets where?
- 3 John 1:5–8. Hospitality worthy of God.

A Peep or Two from You

_____

_____

_____

_____

_____

_____

_____

_____

_____

_____

_____

_____

_____

 WISDOM

"DO NOT FORGET TO ENTERTAIN STRANGERS,

FOR BY SO DOING SOME PEOPLE HAVE

ENTERTAINED ANGELS WITHOUT KNOWING IT."

Hebrews 13:2, NIV

"'IF ANYONE GIVES EVEN A CUP OF COLD WATER

TO ONE OF THESE LITTLE ONES BECAUSE HE IS MY DISCIPLE, I TELL YOU

THE TRUTH, HE WILL CERTAINLY NOT LOSE HIS REWARD.'"

Matthew 10:42, NIV

"To focus on the negative or
bothersome habits of another is to waste time
in which love could grow."

EDITH SCHAEFFER

 SISTERCHICKIN' SUGGESTIONS

Got time for tea? Invite a friend or two to your home, and include
someone new from your church or neighborhood. Keep it simple.
Just offer what you have from your heart. Let your friends bring
their favorite treats to add to the menu. Also ask them to bring
menus or directions to their favorite restaurants in town as well
as fliers from local points of interest to give to the newcomer.

A New Dream

"You need a new dream. A fresh start.
Something wonderful to look forward to."
—LAURIE, *SISTERCHICKS DO THE HULA!*

I loved him; he loved me. He bought me an engagement ring; I bought a wedding dress. We set a date and selected invitations. Then, on a cold afternoon in February, he looked me in the eye and said he didn't think it was going to work out. He probably was right. Although, as a twenty-one-year-old, I couldn't possibly see that while sitting alone, holding close all the fragments of my broken heart.

My closest friend, Luanne, came to be with me the night of my disengagement. She took me out to eat, but of course I couldn't eat. Instead of hamburgers and fries at Coco's, Luanne fed me words.

"You need a new dream. A fresh start. Something to look forward to."

By the time we left the restaurant, Luanne and I had formed a plan to get our fresh starts in Europe together that summer. Those amazing months abroad expanded my view of God, of who I was, and of how my life might count for eternity. In many ways it was a fledgling Sisterchicks sort of experience, because a passion for travel and new experiences was ignited in me.

When I returned home, I met Ross. Another new dream. A dream that turned into a sweet reality.

Luanne's wise words weren't only for a season. In my early forties, a string of health problems led to a week in the hospital; an extensive surgery; big, ugly scars; and more tests. All was stable for a few years, and then I had more problems and more pesky poking and prodding. This time the diagnosis was malignant.

Some of you know what happens in your spirit when you hear that word. Suddenly you or someone you love are redefined, no longer seemingly invincible. They are marked—finite. All the clichés come at you about the sands in the hourglass of life running out.

When I heard the word *malignant*, I felt an overwhelming sense of loss. I might not be around long enough to see my children marry. I had big dreams about kissing my grandbabies and traveling to Australia someday so I could feed a kangaroo out of my hand.

That's when Luanne's words softly feathered over my spirit. *"You need a new dream. A fresh start. Something to look forward to."*

Heaven would be, after all, the ultimate fresh start. Yet heaven was a place I'd barely considered yet. I was too busy living on this spinning orb. One of my grandmas lived to be ninety-four. Why shouldn't I? My other grandma, however, died at forty. Her malady was similar to my current diagnosis.

Sinking into a lonely sadness, I pondered what it would be like to leave my disease-infested pup tent of a body and trade it in for a new creation body. Instead of packing for a journey on the eve of that disengagement from life, I began to do a sort of unpacking. After all, we take nothing with us. All we need, beginning with Christ, is already in heaven waiting for us.

During one of those curled-up-in-bed-with-the-covers-over-my-head sessions, I realized that a lifetime can easily be spent just organizing all the brokenness and trying to come up with new ways to manage our unremitting sin nature.

In several private conversations with the Lord, my spirit bowed low, and I acquiesced to His plan, His timing, His will. My perspective flipped. Life really was the journey to death. Death really was the journey to life. Heaven was my real home. God said our eyes haven't seen and our ears haven't yet heard all that He has prepared for those who love Him. There is more. So much more. And that "more" can't be experienced on earth in this body. The promise of heaven gently became my new, very real dream.

Another surgery was scheduled. I came out of it with another scar. Unexpectedly, I also was given an "all clear" report from the doctor. It looked as if my excursion to heaven would be postponed until a later, unknown date.

WIT 'N' WHIMSY

"The greatest thing is to be found at one's post as a child of God, living each day as though it were our last, but planning as though our world might last a hundred years."

–C. S. LEWIS, *Into the Wardrobe*

That last surgery took place six years ago, and every year since my blood work has come back clear. My days picked up their usual quick pace with barely a blip in the schedule. I have traveled, lived, and loved more deeply this past half decade than I think I did in all the years preceding the day the "m" word was spoken into my life.

Two years ago I stood in a wildlife park outside Sydney with Cheerios in my palm. The cutest kangaroo in all of Australia hopped over and ate out of my hand. His tongue was dry and quick like a kitten's. His tiny paws rested on the edge of my cupped hand, and he batted his irresistible long lashes at me like a little flirt. I was smitten!

The strangely beautiful thing is that I "live" a wonderful life. Yet I know this isn't going to work out, so to speak. This body is destined to decay. I am finite. I am made for something bigger. Something eternal. Deep inside I carry a longing for a new dream, a dream far outside this deficient flesh. It is the quiet dream of heaven.

My soul is unpacked and ready to go.

Until then I will string together many small dreams of what God has waiting for us there. I mean, if He thought up kangaroos for this planet, what has He thought up for heaven? Eyes haven't yet seen. Ears haven't yet heard. The stories haven't yet been told.

Just as Luanne gave words of hope to a heartbroken Robin, Sisterchicks everywhere link arms and steady each other when dreams falter or die. While one grieves, the other keeps a lookout for new hope. Then we go on together, changed, sometimes with borrowed courage, toward what God will bring next.

Each of us has our own stories of broken dreams and new beginnings. What are yours? Who walked with you into a different future than you had imagined? What are some of the treasures God has shown you on this new path?

Long ago, in a faraway land, a widow held out new hope for her widowed daughter-in-law. Naomi said to Ruth, "My dear daughter, isn't it about time I arranged a good home for you so you can have a happy life?" (Ruth 3:1).

Naomi set right to work, and before Ruth knew it, she was married to a wonderful man named Boaz. Ruth and Boaz had a famous great-grandson, David, king of Israel. Generations later, another grandson was born to their family line. His name was Jesus.

All our hopes and dreams for here and for eternity are found in Jesus. Someday each of us will unpack all that we hold on to here. We'll leave our less-than-dependable bodies, along with all the clothes, makeup, and dustibles—oops, collectibles—with which we so carefully surround ourselves. We'll enter heaven empty-handed and find that everything we need is ready for us.

Until then, let's walk beside hurting friends and courageously seek out different yet still wonderful dreams here. Let's believe together the words of Paul the apostle: "For to me, to live is Christ and to die is gain" (Philippians 1:21, NIV).

TAKE A CLOSER LOOK

- Psalm 73:25. This is the right attitude!
- John 14:2–3. There's plenty of room in God's house.
- Philippians 3:20–21. Now that's a trade worth making!

A Peep or Two from You

_____

_____

_____

_____

_____

_____

_____

_____

_____

_____

 WISDOM

"ALL PRAISE TO THE GOD AND FATHER OF OUR MASTER,
JESUS THE MESSIAH! FATHER OF ALL MERCY!
GOD OF ALL HEALING COUNSEL! HE COMES ALONGSIDE US
WHEN WE GO THROUGH HARD TIMES, AND BEFORE YOU KNOW IT,
HE BRINGS US ALONGSIDE SOMEONE ELSE WHO IS GOING THROUGH
HARD TIMES SO THAT WE CAN BE THERE FOR THAT PERSON
JUST AS GOD WAS THERE FOR US."

2 Corinthians 1:3−4

QUOTABLE SISTERCHICKS

"If we had no winter, the spring would not be so
pleasant. If we did not sometimes taste adversity,
prosperity would not be so welcome."

ANNE BRADSTREET, A PURITAN
WHO BECAME THE AUTHOR OF THE FIRST PUBLISHED
BOOK OF POETRY BY AN AMERICAN

Operation "Link Arms"

Make a date for coffee with a friend who needs a new dream. Listening is the first language of loving, so plan to spend most of your time listening. Offer her the encouragement God has offered you in your own hard times, and pray for her. Then plan another outing to a fun movie or for an evening with a group of friends.

Enter His gates with thanksgiving and His courts with praise.

On a Wing and a Prayer

*"My heart has heard you say,
'Come and talk with me.'
And my heart responds,
'LORD, I am coming.'"*

PSALM 27:8, NLT

*"I would rather walk with God in the dark
than go alone in the light."*

MARY GARDINER BRAINARD

Dark-Winged Guilt

*"When that dark-winged vulture guilt swoops in
on the roof of your psyche, tell it to go fly."*
—SHARON, *SISTERCHICKS ON THE LOOSE!*

Last week was awful. Just awful. I was trying to accomplish three weeks' worth of stuff in three days. Everything I put my hand to turned complicated. You know the sort of week I'm talking about. Every unfinished task was linked to something that needed to be taken care of first; so instead of dividing my problems, I multiplied them.

Each night I tumbled into bed (two hours later than when I'd promised myself I'd turn in), certain I had accomplished nothing all day. I was sure I'd have nightmares about my foreboding "Must Do" list.

By day four of this crazy-making, I dashed out the door to an important meeting. Halfway there, I realized I had left some necessary papers at home. I was already late, so I didn't turn around and go back. Instead I tried to slip into the meeting and appear ready for the discussion.

Then the nicest thing happened. Paula was there. Paula, who had been to China, India, and Venezuela and can sing jingles from vintage commercials on demand. Paula, who is my unfailing friend and bringer of truth and hope.

She made a place at the table and looped me into the conversation. She made me feel as if I really did belong.

After the meeting was over, I turned to her and said, "Thanks for being so welcoming even after I got here late. Really, thanks. You have no idea what a train wreck I have been these past few days..."

Paula listened as I vented, and then she calmly said, as if quoting from some source I should recognize, "She did what she could."

"Are you recommending a line for my tombstone? Because if the rest of the week continues at this velocity, you'll no doubt be called upon to write my epitaph before long."

"Actually, I was quoting Jesus. Look it up. Mark chapter 14."

I intended to make a beeline for my Bible as soon as I arrived home. But you know that didn't happen. I had to stop at the grocery store, and of course the phone was ringing as I pulled into the driveway, and well, I'm sure you can picture from personal experience how the rest of the evening went.

That night I cried. I was so far behind on everything. The pressure hadn't let up. The silent accusations pounded on my spirit with heavy

> ### WIT 'N' WHIMSY
>
> **How many times is multitasking mentioned in the Bible? Not even once!**
>
> **Mothers fight all their lives against dirt, and when they die, they are buried in it.**
>
> –ANONYMOUS

fists, slugging their impressions into me with each blow. *You are a mess. You don't know what you're doing. You are such a failure. What a disappointment you are to so many people who have been depending on you.* On it went until spiritual and physical exhaustion took over.

I woke when it was still dark. If I could have fallen back to sleep, I would have. Instead I prayed. More accurately, I "splayed." That's what often happens when I'm faced all over again with the realization of how desperately I need a Savior. When I fall on my knees and smash open my soul before the Lord, it's not a tidy event. The contents of my frail heart gush out all over the throne room of heaven.

In an effort to confine my "splaying" to a private experience, I got out of bed. My husband didn't hear me totter downstairs, going off to meet the Lord in the middle of the night.

I thought again of Paula's verse and found it, just like she said. Matthew, Mark, and John all wrote an account of a woman who "splayed" herself in front of God. She broke open her alabaster jar of expensive perfume at the feet of her Savior and immediately experienced criticism. Immediately!

The perfume, they said, could have been sold and the money used to feed the poor. In other words, she could have done a much better job of managing herself, her resources, and her time.

To those accusers Jesus said, "Leave her alone."

Oh, I love that! "Leave her alone." You tell 'em, Lord!

He then said, "She has done a beautiful thing to me.... She did what she could" (Mark 14:6–8a, NIV).

I knew when I read those powerful statements that I had been listening more attentively to the accuser's taunts during the chaotic first half of the week than I had been to the Lover of my soul. The enemy did in my heart the same thing he has done since the beginning of time: He broke in, stole, and destroyed. Christ, who is my advocate with the Father, defended me.

I underlined those three sentences in my Bible and copied them on a note card. As the new day began, a newness began in me. Nothing about my situation had changed. The pressure was still there. But the pouring out of my shattered spirit before the Lord had turned the mess of my life into a beautiful, fragrant mess. Jesus told my accusers to leave me alone. I was participating in something womanly and ancient that was beautiful to Him. He knew and I knew that I did what I could.

Standing ankle-deep in "splayed" alabaster prayers, I told that old dark-winged vulture guilt to go fly.

And he had to.

*H*as that dark-winged vulture guilt told you lies? Girlfriend, it's time to inform that old buzzard, "You are sooo not welcome here!"

Perhaps you feel due for a "splaying" session with the Lord. He is ready, willing, and able to hear you. Writing down your thoughts and feelings can add clarity and give you a safe place to store them while you wait for the Lord to help you sort them out.

Suppose a friend came to you with feelings of inadequacy and guilt. What encouragement would you give her? Listen to what Jesus said:

> "Are you tired? Worn out? Burned out on religion? Come
> to me. Get away with me and you'll recover your life. I'll
> show you how to take a real rest. Walk with me and work
> with me—watch how I do it. Learn the unforced rhythms
> of grace. I won't lay anything heavy or ill-fitting on you.
> Keep company with me and you'll learn to live freely and
> lightly." (Matthew 11:28–30)

As you reflect on these verses, what does God's Spirit say to your heart? As you lay your daily responsibilities before the Lord, do you feel new freedom to let any of them go? Whether you can make changes or not, what gives you encouragement and peace in the verses above?

Here's a little test to determine the origin of negative thoughts. Remember that the enemy accuses and condemns us. The end result is a greater distance from God. But the Spirit of God comes quietly, speaks gently, and points us to Jesus. When the Holy Spirit helps us to see our sin, the end result is forgiveness, hope, and renewed closeness with God the Father.

Examine the "voices" in your head; do they accuse and condemn, or do they speak gently and remind you of God's love for you? Do they bring you closer to God or pull you away from Him? When you understand the source, you're better equipped to tell guilt and shame to fly or to embrace the forgiveness and hope that Christ offers.

As you fly through this week, may you feel freshly encouraged to do what you can. Perhaps you will hear the Lord whisper to the accuser, "Leave her alone.... She has done a beautiful thing to me.... She did what she could."

TAKE A CLOSER LOOK

- Romans 8:1. Yeah, no condemnation!
- Colossians 1:9–12. Watch how God works.
- 1 John 3:18–20. For when our hearts condemn us.

A Peep or Two from You

_____

_____

_____

_____

_____

_____

_____

_____

_____

_____

_____

_____

_____

WISDOM

"ONCE THE COMMITMENT IS CLEAR, YOU DO WHAT YOU CAN,

NOT WHAT YOU CAN'T. THE HEART REGULATES THE HANDS."

2 Corinthians 8:12

"BUT JESUS SAID, 'LET HER ALONE. WHY ARE YOU GIVING HER A HARD TIME? SHE HAS JUST DONE SOMETHING WONDERFULLY SIGNIFICANT FOR ME. YOU WILL HAVE THE POOR WITH YOU EVERY DAY FOR THE REST OF YOUR LIVES. WHENEVER YOU FEEL LIKE IT, YOU CAN DO SOMETHING FOR THEM. NOT SO WITH ME. SHE DID WHAT SHE COULD WHEN SHE COULD—SHE PRE-ANOINTED MY BODY FOR BURIAL. AND YOU CAN BE SURE THAT WHEREVER IN THE WHOLE WORLD THE MESSAGE IS PREACHED, WHAT SHE JUST DID IS GOING TO BE TALKED ABOUT ADMIRINGLY.'"

Mark 14:6–9

QUOTABLE SISTERCHICKS

"There was once a king sitting on his throne....
It pleased the king to raise a small feather
from the ground and he commanded it to fly.
The feather flew, not because of anything in itself
but because the air bore it along.
Thus am I, a feather on the breath of God."

ABBESS HILDEGARD OF BINGEN,
A FEATHER ON THE BREATH OF GOD

Soul-Twins

> *"I wish I could wrap up and give to you
> the gift you've always given me...grace."*
> —SHARON, *SISTERCHICKS ON THE LOOSE!*

he only thing I don't like about my soul-twin, Anne, is the distance from her front door to mine—5,712 miles. I Googled it once. She lives in the Netherlands, and I live in the great Pacific Northwest.

At first, Anne and I didn't want to be friends. That's not what she says now, but it's true. When we first met at an international book fair in Frankfurt, Germany, neither of us was looking for a new friend. I think we both had the same first impression: We were too different to be fast friends. But we made that assumption because we hadn't compared grace-stories.

Anne was raised in the Pacific Northwest, then graduated from Stanford University in California. I was raised in California and then moved to the Northwest. She traveled to Europe the same summer I did. I came home, married, and had two babies. Anne returned to Europe, married a Dutchman, and had two babies. Both of us wrote a dozen children's book projects while our children were young. We wrote our first novels at the same age. Anne has a passion for travel and world-class dark chocolate. So do I, baby. Oh yeah, so do I.

Oh, and we share the same middle name. An uncommon name, spelled the same way even. (No, I'm not going to tell you what it is.)

For the past decade, a stream of tandem publishing and book promotion opportunities has given Anne and me glorious excuses to be together. We have connected in Toronto for ribbon-cutting ceremonies, Denver for book trade shows, and Cambridge, England, to co-teach a fiction workshop. We even met up in Paris a few summers ago, where our husbands joined us for an unforgettable weekend that included a five-hour dinner at Anne's favorite restaurant. One year in Orlando, Anne and I rented a convertible and drove to our television interview with the top down and the music blaring. She said we were Sisterchicks on the loose, and I suddenly had the title for the book I was writing at the time.

When Anne travels by herself, she goes quietly and looks for stories of hope. Her passport includes visa stamps from Russia, Mozambique, Bosnia, Liberia, and Iraq. She slips into these places of darkness and captures truth in a butterfly net. Then, with all her heart, she attempts to bring this vivid honesty back to Western culture while the story's fragile wings still are fluttering. Anne's books display her collection of captured truths. She wins awards, and when she stands behind a podium to speak, the audience barely breathes, barely blinks.

I've tried to figure out what it is that makes some friendships blossom while others wilt on the vine. I don't know why exactly, but with Anne I know it has something to do with our stories. Not the stories we write, because we are quite opposite in that realm. I mean the grace-stories of our lives that are being written by the Author and Finisher of our faith. He pens each with His unique creativity and wild sovereignty. When we share our stories, something eternal happens.

At least that's what happened a number of years ago when Anne and I were still testing our fledgling friendship. We made plans to meet up at London's Heathrow Airport and clambered into an express coach headed for Oxford, happy to have a few November days together. It was a "Selah" (a word from the Psalms that means "pause and think on that") sort of moment squeezed in between other business, writing, and travel. A poetic chance to reflect and breathe.

Our Saturday morning arrival in Oxford allowed us a full afternoon to explore. We tromped down to the edge of the Cherwell River, where flatboats could be hired to go punting. The man in charge wouldn't rent a boat to Anne and me. He said we were "just two women." Punting was a sport for the young. It was an athletic endeavor reserved for strong males.

Is that so?

Anne and I walked away gracefully. We knew better. We knew that between the two of us, we could have hoisted that old geezer and punted *him* down the river!

Instead, we opted for a leisurely perusing of the many antique bookstores near Magdalen College. Oxford, with its sixty colleges and five-hundred-year history of being a place of learning, provided for us shop after shop filled with the musty, intoxicating scent of stories told and stories forgotten. We were unashamed gluttons of such.

Anne suggested we follow our strong story libations with a long late afternoon walk in the autumn air. The trail we found was strewn with orange and yellow newly fallen leaves the size of a giant's hand. Bushels of them floated from the ancient trees, resting a moment on our shoulders before sliding to the woodland carpet and crunching beneath our feet. Gathering up the vibrant beauties in bouquets, we waved them in the air. Hosanna!

Every curve in the trail brought us to new discoveries under the tussled trees along the silvery river on that achingly beautiful afternoon. Piercing shafts of golden light led us farther on and deeper in. Later we found out that we had strolled through Addison's Walk, the same trail C. S. Lewis and J. R. R. Tolkien often took. At the time, all we knew was that the place was enchanting and crowded with kind and listening trees.

On that trail, Anne and I offered to each other the raw and uncut versions of our lives. Anne spoke softly into the moss-scented air, quietly entrusting to me an "unpublished" chapter of her life story. I received her words and responded in kind. What we experienced in the midst of our candid disclosures was something rare and beautiful. Acceptance. The fruit of uncomplicated grace.

As we listened, not a hint of judgment clouded our expressions toward each other. We didn't compare or complain or contrive to be anything we weren't. We just rolled out the truth, and in our receiving of each other's stories, our hearts were knit together.

We walked until we reached a meadow where the sheltering trees ended. Before us, the dreaming spires of Oxford cast a hazy silhouette as twilight came, smoking a pipe. With our fists still clenching the enchanted leaves, we made our way back to town in shared silence.

Somehow we both knew that this was the way soul-twins should spend such an afternoon in such a place. Anne says that afternoon was a gift for both of us. She says that's how it is with God. He gives us unexpected gifts at unexpected times. I believe that's true. Anne and I didn't think we needed a new friend when we met each other. But the Lord knew. And He gave. Unexpectedly.

_F_riendships often come unexpectedly. Right in the middle of ordinary days, God steps in and...as Hope in _Sisterchicks Do the Hula!_ says, "Then as only God can, He surprised me. I think He prompted Laurie to call out of the blue just to prove that He knows me by heart. He knows what I need even when I'm too timid or belligerent to ask for it. Laurie and I had an unfinished dream.... I couldn't explain where all the joy came from. I already had a great life with a wonderful husband and three healthy sons. But now I had Laurie again, and she was filling up a place in my life that had been empty for a long time."

Who has been a soul-sister for you? Describe how God brought you together. Remember one or two special times you shared. How did God bless the two of you?

One of the wonderful characteristics of a true friendship is that it can survive separation, both by time and distance. Consider reconnecting with a dear friend from the past.

Women who share both friendship and faith can have an impact on each other long after they have parted. Take Mary, for example. One day, out of the clear blue, she finds out God has chosen her to carry His Son. She is told that an elderly relative, Elizabeth, is pregnant. A short time later, Mary is at Elizabeth's house. Elizabeth shouts out, "Blessed are you among women, and blessed is the child you will bear!" (Luke 1:42, NIV).

In that one exclamation, Mary receives acceptance and grace deep in her soul. Do you suppose Elizabeth's expression of love comforted Mary in the years ahead, when others viciously reminded each other about her untimely pregnancy?

What encouraging words from a friend still ring in your ears? Is there someone in your life who needs your love and acceptance right now? Wouldn't it be grand if right in the middle of an ordinary day, God surprised that someone with a friendship-touch from you?

He might just wrap up His grace and send it through you.

TAKE A CLOSER LOOK

- Proverbs 18:24. Now this is a friend!
- 1 Samuel 20:42. Here's a forever promise.
- Philippians 4:2–3. Help friends who disagree.

A Peep or Two from You

_____

_____

_____

_____

_____

_____

 WISDOM

"IT'S BETTER TO HAVE A PARTNER THAN GO IT ALONE.

SHARE THE WORK, SHARE THE WEALTH....

BY YOURSELF YOU'RE UNPROTECTED.

WITH A FRIEND YOU CAN FACE THE WORST.

CAN YOU ROUND UP A THIRD?

A THREE-STRANDED ROPE ISN'T EASILY SNAPPED."

Ecclesiastes 4:9, 12

"But oh! The blessing it is to have a friend
to whom one can speak fearless on any subject; with
whom one's deepest as well as one's
most foolish thoughts come out simply and safely. Oh,
the comfort—the inexpressible comfort
of feeling safe with a person—having neither to
weigh thoughts nor measure words,
but pouring them all right out, just as they are,
chaff and grain together; certain that a
faithful hand will take and sift them, keep what is
worth keeping, and then with the
breath of kindness blow the rest away."

DINAH MARIA MULOCK CRAIK, *A LIFE FOR A LIFE*

Treasures in the Dark

FROM ROBIN'S NEST

*"All this means is now you have to trust God
in a bigger way than you did before all this happened."*
— PENNY, *SISTERCHICKS ON THE LOOSE!*

We had a really rough season when our children were young. The details of how we became so shipwrecked aren't essential to repeat at this point. Those of you who have survived debilitating storms in your marriage, your finances, your health, or with your children or careers know what happens to your spirit during those seasons. Part of you becomes very small.

In our shipwrecked season, we had to move in with my parents for seven months. All four of us lived in one room in the basement with the washer and dryer. Our son and daughter were school-age and slept on folding canvas cots my parents used for camping when I was young. Ross and I had their old bed and a dresser. All of our remaining belongings were in storage in another town six hundred miles away. We still had our same vehicle: a van. It was always packed with overflow stuff. We had a small ice chest wedged between the front seats, and our kids had their own area where they could store some of their favorite toys and books. We were all learning to live in a new state of simplicity.

Yes, it was humbling, paralyzing, and frightening to be in such a depleted state. If I didn't have such gracious parents, I'm not sure where we would have lived or what we would have done.

One Sunday we visited a new church. Our son, who badly needed a haircut, bounded out of the car and tore a hole in the knee of his nice pants. He looked like a ragamuffin when I checked him in to Sunday school, but the teacher was kind, and he was happy to be there instead of in "big church."

After the service I went to pick him up from class. He waved to the nice teacher and walked out with a paper in one hand and two cookies in the other.

"The teacher gave me two cookies, Mom! All the other kids only got one, but I got two."

"That was nice of her. Was it because you were new to the class?"

"No, I think it was because of my picture."

"Your picture?"

"We were supposed to draw a picture of where we lived, and when I showed the teacher my picture, she went and got me another cookie."

My son held up his prize picture so I could see.

It was a drawing of our van.

I think that was one of my lowest days. Not because our circumstances were so grim; they weren't. Not really. We had food, shelter, and family that loved us. But I was devastated when I thought of all we were putting our children through with so many moves and so much dissecting of what would be considered "normal" life for an American family. My son had drawn a picture of our van with our four round faces looking out the windows because that had been the only constant in his life for the past year.

My journaling during those months took on a crisp focus on Father God. We were more dependent on Him than we had ever been. I memorized parts of Isaiah 45 and began to murmur the verses in my prayers. "I will give you treasures hidden in the darkness—secret riches. I will do this so you may know that I am the LORD, the God of Israel, the one who calls you by name" (v. 3, NLT).

Even in the compressed anxiousness of my spirit, I wanted to remind God of promises He had made to others centuries ago. Could He not still honor the same sort of promises to our family? Where were the treasures hidden in our darkness? Why were we in this darkness?

The only answer I could find was more of a declaration than an answer. Isaiah quotes God, "I am the one who creates the light and makes the darkness. I am the one who sends good times and bad times. I, the LORD, am the one who does these things" (v. 7, NLT).

My only response echoed Isaiah's: "Truly, O God of Israel, our Savior, you work in strange and mysterious ways" (v. 15, NLT).

That was the only clarity I had. God was God. He could do whatever He wanted. He was giving us an opportunity to trust Him in bigger ways than ever before. That foundation of trust in God alone was essential in holding us together as a couple and as a family in the years that followed.

Of course, I didn't know that at the time.

The shipwrecked season ended, as all shipwreck seasons do. Other storms came and went. Our children are now in their twenties.

A few months ago, the two of them visited my mom in the retirement community where she now lives since Dad passed away. Mom called me a few days later, delighted with the visit from her grown grandchildren.

"Do you know what your children talked about at lunch? They talked about when all of you lived with us up in the mountains."

I cringed. Was this when the therapy bills were going to start coming in for all the years of counseling our children would require after we had bungled their childhoods?

"What did they say?" I asked.

"They have keen memories of the forts they built and the walks they went on with Grandpa. It was very sweet listening to them."

"I was so worried they had been ruined for life."

"Heavens no! Those were happy times for us, for your father and me. Do you know what your children said? They said they think the reason the two of them are close now is because you moved so much when they were young. It meant they had to be friends with each other."

There it was. All these years later and I was still being shown small treasures that were hidden in that darkness. A small yet precious reminder that God is God. He can do whatever He wants. And it seems that what He wants is to draw us closer to His heart so that we will trust Him completely in every season of life, the good times and the bad times. Both come from Him. He does indeed work in strange and mysterious ways.

When we're stumbling around in the darkness of tough times, it helps to have God's promises to hold on to. For thousands of years, believers have held on to this one in Romans: "We know that in all things God works for the good of those who love him, who have been called according to his purpose" (8:28, NIV).

This promise is a soul-deep, Holy Spirit–strong lifeline that brings us to the precious treasures we discover only in a journey through the darkness. One of the greatest treasures is learning to trust God in a bigger way than we did before.

When you look back, can you see God working in His strange and mysterious ways through some of your challenging seasons? What were the unexpected treasures that came out of the darkness?

How comforting to know that nothing comes to us unless it has first passed through God's mind. We'll never hear an "oops" from heaven.

WIT 'N' WHIMSY

"Be comforted, dear soul! There is always light behind the clouds."
–LOUISA MAY ALCOTT, *Little Women*

"If we cannot believe God when circumstances seem to be against us, we do not believe Him at all."
–CHARLES SPURGEON

TAKE A CLOSER LOOK

- Job 1:20–22. No blame for God here!
- Job 42. God restores.
- Isaiah 41:4. God's first and last.

A Peep or Two from You

_____

_____

_____

_____

_____

_____

_____

_____

_____

_____

_____

_____

_____

_____

"'YOU KNOW WITH ALL YOUR HEART AND SOUL

THAT NOT ONE OF ALL THE GOOD PROMISES THE LORD YOUR GOD

GAVE YOU HAS FAILED. EVERY PROMISE HAS BEEN FULFILLED.'"

Joshua 23:14, NIV

"HE [GOD] OPENS UP THE DEPTHS, TELLS SECRETS,

SEES IN THE DARK—LIGHT SPILLS OUT OF HIM!"

Daniel 2:22

SISTERCHICKIN' SUGGESTION

Promise Bouquet

Invite several friends over to bless a friend going through a dark
time. Have a number of fresh flowers and a pretty vase on hand.
Ask each friend to share a promise from the Bible with your
hurting friend. As the promise is shared, tie a small tag to one of
the flowers, put the verse's "address" on it, and place the flower
in the vase. Send your "Promise Bouquet" home to remind your
friend that she is loved and so that she can look up the verses
when she feels the need for further encouragement.

Shimmering Bits

FROM ROBIN'S NEST

"You cast your net on the other side [of the boat],
and look at all the shimmering bits of glory you're pulling in now!"
— PENNY, *SISTERCHICKS ON THE LOOSE!*

When we reach heaven, my best friend, Donna, and I want to introduce you to a woman we met in Latvia. Her name is Marija, and to be honest, neither of us wanted to go to her house to see her. But, oh, what a moment of glory we would have missed!

Donna and I went to Latvia in 1993 to bring chocolate chips and cheer to a young missionary wife. I was invited to speak to the women at a church in the capital city, Riga. After an already full day, our interpreter asked if we would consider going to visit a woman who was ill.

I looked at Donna; she looked at me. We had spent the day sharing our hearts, teaching from the Bible, and standing for hours, listening through an interpreter to dozens of hurting women as they looked to us for any drop of encouragement. Since it now was after nine at night, I was ready to find a few nourishing morsels of food and fall into the nearest bed. Offering my weary self to all the germs of an ill person seemed like a bad idea.

"It's up to you," Donna said, giving me a bedraggled look.

Apparently it wasn't truly up to me, because even though my mind was saying, "Sorry, no," my mouth somehow translated those two simple words into, "Okay, we'll go." What is it the Bible says about the Spirit of God interceding for us? Does He transpose our intentions for us as well?

We were offered a ride to Marija's house so we wouldn't have to depend on the public tram. Unfortunately, the hospitality offered exceeded the maximum load capacity available. Like a troupe of circus clowns, we smushed seven bodies into a Soviet sedan built for four.

"You're squashing me," I murmured into the back of Donna's head. She was smaller and hence given the princess position on my lap.

"You're hogging all the legroom," she countered under her breath.

"Am not. Stop jiggling."

"I'm not jiggling. It's the road, or should I say, the ruts in the road?"

Our interpreter squeezed a peek at us from her two-to-a-front-seat position. "All is okay?"

I'd forgotten that anyone else in the car spoke English and could understand our squabbling. Donna and I have been known to have our feisty moments. We've found that exchanging dialogue as if we were childhood sibling rivals defuses tension. Our interpreter, however, didn't know that.

"All is okay?" she asked again. "We have only another ten minutes to drive."

"Ten minutes?" I groaned, feeling my legs going numb.

"This was your idea," Donna muttered.

I would have pinched her accessible backside, but my hand was wedged behind the door handle.

Our ten-minute ride turned into twenty minutes. I felt as if we were being kidnapped. The dark skies hurled javelins of lightning followed by roars of thunder. Apparently Donna and I weren't the only two elements having a spat that night.

The clown car came to an abrupt stop in front of a dilapidated manor that I felt I'd seen before—when I had toured a Hollywood studio and viewed a set for the original Addams Family show. Or was it the Munsters?

Big drops of rain pelted us as we performed a series of unattractive contortions to extract our bodies from the car. I opened my travel umbrella, but a gust of wind popped it inside out. Nothing about this moment felt good.

We dashed to the front door, where a flickering overhead light welcomed us. I held my breath. Not because I expected to be greeted by Cousin Itt, but because it smelled awful. Like dead cats. The woman who opened to our late-night knock wasn't Morticia, but Marija's full-time caregiver. She ushered us quietly into what had once been the dining room of this large house. In typical Communist fashion, the upstairs and downstairs had been converted into many cubicles of space with a separate family occupying each cubicle.

Tentatively approaching the corner, where a single lamp was lit, we came as close as we dared to the narrow bed where the diminished invalid sat, propped up by a pillow. Her white hair was clean and combed back from her glowing face. I hadn't expected Marija to be so astonishingly beautiful.

At first I wondered if the dim light on this elderly woman's pale skin gave her such a glow. Or did she have a fever? A contagious sort of fever that made her look rosy, vital, and yet oh so infectious?

She stretched out her right hand, eager to greet us, to touch us. Her fingers curled in, her wrist was bent. Yet she smiled radiantly. Donna and I hung back, waving our hellos rather than making contact with her. Then I noticed that Marija had no lumps under the covers where her legs should have been. Her left hand lay motionless at her side.

Marija wasn't sick. She had contracted polio forty years ago, when part of the remedy included amputation.

Donna and I were offered two of the three wobbly straight-backed chairs available. Marija began at once to roll out her grace-story for us. Our interpreter could barely keep up as Marija described her losses: a baby at birth, another child in his toddler years, and her husband soon after he was drafted into the Russian army. By the time she was twenty-two, Marija had lost almost everything. Then the polio came and took her legs.

The demure woman spoke softly, with her chin down, as she described how angry she had been with God and how deep the darkness that seemed to swallow her for several years. Then she asked God a question. Not a "why" question, but a "what" question. "What can I possibly do for You now? I am of no use."

And God answered her.

I looked at the others. They didn't blink at her statement. This woman said God answered her. He spoke to her. Was that why her countenance glowed? What does God say to such a small, broken woman on the other side of the world?

With clear, honest eyes, Marija spoke, and her answer was translated. "God told me He took my legs so I would not run around on this earth. Nearly anyone can do that. He asked me to do something different for Him. Something special. Something not everyone can do. He asked me to run every day between this earth and heaven and to carry up to Him the heart cries of His children. This is my job. My purpose. I run to heaven every day."

The room became very still. Donna and I sat with tears shimmering in our eyes, unashamed to let them fall without a sound onto our folded hands in our laps. I found it easy to believe that every time Marija stepped into those courts of heaven, she returned to earth with a bit of glory dust on her face. That was why she glowed.

Our interpreter went on to add that Marija used her crippled hand to write letters to encourage believers around the world. She wrote to Corrie ten Boom once, and Corrie, via an interpreter, wrote her back.

Marija's eyes twinkled at the name Corrie ten Boom. I had met Corrie in California, and that was why Marija wanted to meet me. I worked for a ministry organization that handled all of Corrie's correspondence during the year *The Hiding Place*, the movie about her life in a concentration camp during World War II, was released.

Marija pulled the crumpled letter from under her pillow and reached out her hand to show it to me. One of her most treasured possessions was this letter from Corrie, a woman who knew what it was like to be swallowed by darkness.

Oh, what a gift Donna and I would have missed if we hadn't been willing to "cast our nets on the other side," so to speak, of our schedule and energy to visit Marija. We're still feeding off the shimmering bits of glory pulled up during that exchange.

When it was time to go, Donna and I stood and went over to Marija to curl our arms around her. I pressed my cheek against hers and whispered a blessing, sealing it with a kiss on that rosy, glowing face. She drank it in and blessed me back, promising to pray for Donna and me every day.

Then one November morning, two years after we kissed Marija's face, she made her daily run to heaven, and this time Jesus told her she could stay.

*O*h, Marija, what a picture of grace your life was! You give all of us a new perspective on the struggles we face each day.

Nearly all of us have found ourselves in situations in which we felt like the pregnant woman who wishes she could skip that whole delivery thing. You know, no way out but the way we would prefer to avoid. None of us wants to suffer pain or loss of any kind. We don't ask for something like a physical disability or a lifelong battle with mental illness. But when life's overwhelming challenges come, the only road available is the one that goes right through the pain.

Have you been around someone who has been through some dark valleys? How did that person's experience change your perspective on your life circumstances?

With the blessings of Marija's daily trips to heaven on the wings of prayer, she glowed like an otherworldly saint. But when we see her losses and pain, her oh so normal bout with depression and anger, we know she is one of us.

Has there been a time when you found yourself feeling angry with God or others over your circumstances? For most of us, anger is an unavoidable place to travel through during tough times. While we may not be able to avoid visiting "anger," we certainly don't want to make it our permanent address!

In His kindness to us, the Lord says, "Go ahead and be angry. You do well to be angry—but don't use your anger as fuel for revenge. And don't stay angry. Don't go to bed angry. Don't give the Devil that kind of foothold in your life" (Ephesians 4:26–27).

When we choose to push beyond the anger, through the gate of surrender, we find the peace and joy that initially seemed impossible. Marija surrendered her anger to God, and she glowed. Well, guess what? So can we! This is how it happens: "Do everything without complaining or arguing, so that you may become blameless and pure, children of God without fault in a crooked and depraved generation, in which you shine like stars in the universe as you hold out the word of life" (Philippians 2:14–16, NIV).

So, go ahead—you glow, girl!

Whoa...it's getting shimmery bright in here! Glory!

Take a Closer Look

- Psalm 91:14–16. Hold on for dear life.
- Daniel 12:3. More shining and glowing.
- 2 Corinthians 1:8–12. A reason for hope for those in need.

A Peep or Two from You

_____

_____

_____

_____

_____

_____

_____

_____

_____

 WISDOM

"CONSIDER IT A SHEER GIFT, FRIENDS,

WHEN TESTS AND CHALLENGES COME AT YOU FROM ALL SIDES.

YOU KNOW THAT UNDER PRESSURE, YOUR FAITH-LIFE IS FORCED INTO

THE OPEN AND SHOWS ITS TRUE COLORS. SO DON'T TRY TO

GET OUT OF ANYTHING PREMATURELY. LET IT DO ITS WORK SO YOU

BECOME MATURE AND WELL-DEVELOPED, NOT DEFICIENT IN ANY WAY."

James 1:2—4

"Make sure that you let God's grace work
in your souls by accepting whatever
He gives you, and giving Him whatever
He takes from you. True holiness consists
in doing God's work with a smile."

MOTHER TERESA OF CALCUTTA

I'd give anything for a warm, dry nest and a hot cup of worms (or tea).

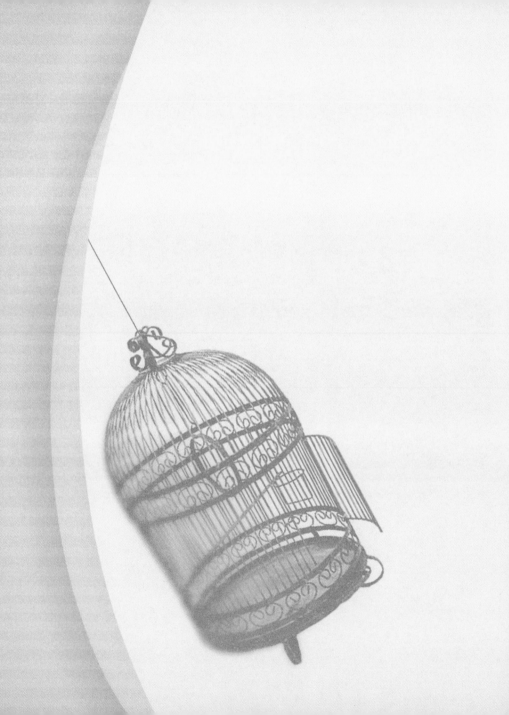

Take a Flying Leap

*"Make a careful exploration of who you are
and the work you have been given,
and then sink yourself into that. Don't be
impressed with yourself. Don't compare
yourself with others. Each of you must
take responsibility for doing the creative best
you can with your own life."*

GALATIANS 6:4–5

*"Give me the love that leads the way,
The faith that nothing can dismay,
The hope no disappointments tire,
The passion that will burn like fire,
Let me not sink to be a clod:
Make me Thy fuel, Flame of God."*

AMY CARMICHAEL

Never Too Late

FROM ROBIN'S NEST

"You have to try new things while you can. You have to tell yourself you can do anything. Otherwise you'll get old fast."

—LAURIE, *SISTERCHICKS DO THE HULA!*

My husband has an aunt we call Aunt Becky, even though her real name is Esther. Becky fits her better. She taught kindergarten in Malibu, California, for thirty-nine years and became a widow in her midforties.

Aunt Becky, who is in her mideighties, lives by herself, eats sushi, and even has a computer she knows how to use. She loves a good party and threw a doozy of a good time on her seventieth birthday.

My daughter, Rachel, and her cousin Alyssa were caught whispering behind the gift table at the big birthday bash. They had just watched Aunt Becky delightfully throw her arms around an elderly gentleman who arrived bearing a potted plant.

"Mom, did you see that? Aunt Becky kissed that man on the lips. Look at him. He has really, really red lips now!" The cousins dissolved in a puddle of preadolescent giggles and were not seen again until it was time for cake.

When Aunt Becky turned eighty, she sent out invitations for another grand birthday celebration. Her plans were a bit more conservative this time, though. She only invited 150 guests.

Our family made the trek to Southern California for the event, arriving a day early to help with details such as picking up the cake and flowers. The morning of the bash, Aunt Becky asked me to come early and help with her makeup. She took a seat at her built-in vanity table. Lined up in front of us was a parade of brand new bottles of lotions and potions, along with a complete palette of eye shadow. The blush and lipstick were in "sizzling summer shades."

"Aunt Becky, where did you get all this new makeup?" I asked.

"At the mall. I went in for a consultation earlier this week and decided it was time to try something new. Now, be sure to do the lip liner before you put on my lipstick."

I got her all dolled up for the party and stood close as she enthusiastically greeted her guests with "sizzling summer" kisses. The tube of replenishment lipstick was in my pocket, ready whenever she called for a touch-up.

This time the cousins weren't giggling as they watched Aunt Becky smooch her guests.

WIT 'N' WHIMSY

"Life is not a journey to the grave with the intention of arriving safely in a pretty and well-preserved body. But rather to skid in broadside, thoroughly used up, totally worn out, and loudly proclaiming, 'Wow! What a ride!'"

–ANONYMOUS

At twenty, the young women viewed her with what I interpreted as tender reverence. Their Aunt Becky was eighty, and she still had *it*. How does a woman do that?

With Aunt Becky, the secret to maintaining the *it* factor has something to do with keeping a young heart. I think she does this, in part, by not being afraid to try new things.

Last fall, Aunt Becky was invited to go on a cruise through the Panama Canal with her friend Margaret. A few weeks before the departure, Aunt Becky injured her knee and was given doctor's orders to use a walker. My sister-in-law took Aunt Becky out "equipment" shopping. Instead of returning with a walker or a cane, however, they came home with a cherry red motorized cart, complete with a basket and an extra battery pack.

My twenty-four-year-old son joined in the outfitting of the new "convertible" and had a small license plate made with the words "Becky's Buggy." When he went over to Aunt Becky's to surprise her with the little gift, he decided to help out by building a skateboard-style ramp in her driveway so she could scoot back and forth to the mailbox. All the neighbors came out to watch Aunt Becky navigate her cul-de-sac, applauding every time she made the "jump" on the skateboard ramp.

However, when Margaret saw the smart little red convertible Aunt Becky was bringing with her on the cruise, she was leery of what other travelers might think. Traveling with "equipment" might make them appear older than they were. Margaret, by the way, is ninety-three.

I thought about Aunt Becky a lot while she was on the cruise and called her a few days after she returned. She said her snappy equipment turned out to be a great conversation starter with the other cruisers. And guess what? Even Margaret took Becky's Buggy out for a spin on the promenade deck.

My friend Anne has a great saying that Aunt Becky's life demonstrates: "Don't let fear make the decisions for you." I think her adage applies at any age. Why live a small life in constant fear of what might go wrong? Go ahead. Try something new.

And make sure you always have your tube of sizzling summer lipstick in your back pocket.

*I*t's never too late to try new things. Aunt Becky proves it.

Sisterchick Rhea followed in that tradition when she decided to sail across the Pacific Ocean on a thirty-nine-foot trimaran when she was in her sixties. Even though she is a weak swimmer, fear didn't dictate her decision.

For Barbara, the challenge came at age seventy-six, when she was invited to stand in front of a large group of women and give a presentation on her years of quilting.

Then there's Irene who, with hope firmly in place, took a coupon to the drugstore and bought antiwrinkle cream at age ninety-six. As she walked away she was heard saying, "I hope it works!"

How do women stay hopeful and vibrant? What comes to mind when you think of the wise, spunky, or fun older women in your world? Have they always had these tendencies, or has there been a dramatic change at some point?

What about you? What three words would you want to describe you when you are in your seventies, eighties, or nineties? Can you tell if you are already on your way to being that kind of woman, or will you have to make dramatic changes?

We can't let Aunt Becky have all the fun! What delightful, scary, or challenging new thing has been sitting in the back of your heart, waiting to be given permission to take flight? Review the roadblocks you see, and decide if they are final or just bumps on the runway to takeoff.

Come on, girls! Let's choose to keep hope alive! Let's dream big dreams until we wake up in heaven, when our best dream becomes reality.

Until then, look for us on the promenade deck with shimmering summer sizzle lipstick in one hand and antiwrinkle cream in the other.

TAKE A CLOSER LOOK

- Psalm 92:12–15. Ever green.
- Luke 1:36. Old and pregnant!
- Luke 2:36–38. Aged Anna still serving God.

A Peep or Two from You

_____

_____

_____

_____

_____

_____

_____

_____

 Wisdom

"But those who hope in the Lord
will renew their strength.
They will soar on wings like eagles;
they will run and not grow weary,
they will walk and not be faint."

Isaiah 40:31, NIV

"Therefore we do not lose heart.
Though outwardly we
are wasting away, yet inwardly we are
being renewed day by day."

2 Corinthians 4:16, NIV

QUOTABLE SISTERCHICKS

"How many blessings I enjoy,
That other people don't.
To weep and sigh because I'm blind,
I cannot and I won't."

FANNY CROSBY, WHO WROTE EIGHT THOUSAND HYMNS.
HER FIRST HYMN WAS PENNED AT THE AGE OF FORTY-FOUR.

"Life is what we make it,
always has been, always will be."

GRANDMA MOSES (AKA ANNA MARY ROBERTSON, 1860–1961)
BEGAN PAINTING IN HER SEVENTIES.
HER PAINTINGS ARE DISPLAYED IN PRESTIGIOUS ART
GALLERIES WORLDWIDE AND ARE IN HIGH DEMAND.

SISTERCHICKIN' SUGGESTION

Ready to try something new? Convince your most
adventuresome friend to take a class at the local
community college with you. Candle making, anyone?
How about tap dancing? Haiku poetry?

Gifted Beyond

FROM ROBIN'S NEST

"You are gifted and capable beyond your wildest imagination.
Drop your bucket deep into the well of possibilities,
and see what you pull up."

— PENNY, *SISTERCHICKS ON THE LOOSE!*

My sister, Julie, is only sixteen months older than I, but she always has been light-years ahead in creativity and ability. However, she got stuck.

I told her this. Several times. With a variety of examples to illuminate my point. Perhaps you know how well such comments tend to go over when delivered by a little sister who doesn't have much tact. Yeah. Like that.

I dropped my goal of creating an extreme-makeover-your-sister program. The episode I had planned lacked one vital component—a willing contestant.

So picture, if you will, the swelling of my bitten tongue when my sister called last fall to tell me that she had been let go from her job.

The job where she had never, in more than half a decade, been invited to make full use of her amazing gifts and abilities.

I made those soft cooing sounds we all want to hear when in search of a sympathetic ear. Then I invited her to go with me to a large women's conference on the other side of the continent. She needed a break. I needed another face-to-face opportunity to unveil my fail-safe plan for her future. As I saw it, the Holy Spirit could take a little break because I would handle this one for Him.

I mean, really. What sister doesn't know best?

Fourteen thousand women were in attendance at this conference. Julie and I were only two of them. I wasn't there to speak or sing or dance. My very small part was to sit at a table in the concourse during the breaks, smile, and sign copies of a novel I'd written specifically for this group.

One of the gestures of generous hospitality from the organizers was to allow Julie and me to be included in the VIP section. We were assigned seats right up front and were ushered to the greenroom backstage before the event began.

Only half a dozen other women were in the greenroom when Julie and I entered and went through a buffet line for the catered meal. I had coached Julie ahead of time on the routine of making ourselves invisible once we were in close quarters with these Very Important Women. After all, these speakers and singers were being used by God in mighty ways. They were the heart of the gig. My sister and I were the silent, humbly honored guests.

Julie knew only too well how to be invisible. She and I sat at the table in the corner and ate quietly.

I love what transpired next because it happened so softly. So effortlessly. The Spirit of God gently matched His remedy to the wound hidden in my sister's soul. The wound I could sense but couldn't see or touch.

One of the highly honored women came over to our table and said a warm hello to me since we had met before. Then she introduced herself to my sister. The woman didn't need to tell Julie who she was. She was that famous. In twenty minutes, this powerful woman was going to stand on the stage in front of those fourteen thousand women and do what she was gifted by God to do. She was going to minister in a big way.

At that moment, however, she smiled at my sister. "Would you like something to drink? I notice you didn't get a beverage."

"No, that's okay. You don't have to. I can get something."

Before my flustered sister could finish speaking, this pillar-of-the-faith woman slipped over to the beverage table and returned with a cold bottle of water for Julie. Then she sat down and talked with us. You know, girlfriend chat, like we were all equal at the foot of the cross. No celebrities here. Only sisters.

That one sweetly simple act—a cup of cold water in Jesus' name—flew in the face of a lie Julie had believed for far too long. Here was the truth, in a living, breathing demonstration. Julie was of great value in the sight of God and the sight of others.

Funny, isn't it, how some truths are so hidden from us? We can see what a lie does in a heart and a life, but until God makes it clear to the injured person what that soul wound is, no hodgepodge home remedy will fix the problem.

That night Julie and I stayed up late talking, each of us ensconced in her bed the way we did when we were young. I asked my sister what she wanted to do. This was a switch from announcing all the great ideas I had for her life.

"Flowers," she said without hesitation.

For many years Julie had created everything that made weddings beautiful. She could do it all—sew the gowns, decorate the cake, arrange the flowers. She loves arranging the flowers.

"That's what you should do," I said.

"I know, but..." Julie's list of obstacles was long.

Apparently the rope on God's possibility bucket is even longer. When He is ready to do a new thing in a willing heart, that bucket can go to the bottom of the well. Julie and I pulled together through the night until that bucket made it all the way up, brimming with options.

Not long after our weekend together, Julie received a small purse embroidered with the words "Dream, Wish, Hope." Inside was tucked some money—dream seeds to pray over and plant.

She cried. Then she gathered all her courage and used the money to enroll in a floral design course at a nearby university.

Last week Julie called me, and this time I was the one who cried. She said she had a new job. At a floral shop. And what's more, the owner told her she was gifted.

As the tenderhearted, supportive little sister I am, I couldn't resist the chance to say, "Told you so."

an't you just picture Julie among her flowers! Do you suppose there are moments when she glows with the joy that comes from knowing her priceless worth to God? Julie has always been of great worth to God and those around her; she just has a clearer sense of that now.

We frequently need a fresh view of our worth. He tells us that we are His work of art. Not just something pretty to set on the shelf, but beautifully crafted to do "good works" that God planned just for us! Check this out if you're in doubt: "For we are God's workmanship, created in Christ Jesus to do good works, which God prepared in advance for us to do" (Ephesians 2:10, NIV).

Our value isn't determined by the opinion of our family, our friends, or even ourselves. Neither is our value determined by our physical attributes, intelligence, how much of the Bible we know, or how many hours of Sunday school we teach. Our value and worth are rooted in God's character and what He says about us, His children.

Can you see ways that you have allowed others to influence your sense of personal worth? God values us because He wants to. That's a real mind bender in a world addicted to achievement.

How could this truth influence your view of yourself? Your view of God? Your view of others? Are you beginning to see some of the lies that you have believed about your worth? The Lord always is ready to replace a lie with His truth.

Can you remember a time when were you treated like a person of worth? How did that make you feel?

Now, take a step back. Look at those around you. Whom do you see that needs to discover that he or she is a priceless work of art that God cherishes? What can you do to help that person believe this great truth? Your gift to him or her could be as simple as a glass of cold water.

TAKE A CLOSER LOOK

- Ephesians 2:6-7. God has us right where He wants us.
- Ephesians 3:20. In your wildest dreams!
- Romans 12:1. Giving God your all.

A Peep or Two from You

_____

_____

_____

_____

_____

_____

_____

_____

WISDOM

"SO BE CONTENT WITH WHO YOU ARE, AND DON'T PUT ON AIRS.
GOD'S STRONG HAND IS ON YOU; HE'LL PROMOTE YOU AT THE RIGHT
TIME. LIVE CAREFREE BEFORE GOD; HE IS MOST CAREFUL WITH YOU."

1 Peter 5:6—7

SISTERCHICKIN' SUGGESTIONS

A Birthday Blessing Blowout

The next time one of the women in your small circle of friends
has a birthday, why not host a little party to honor her? Prepare a
few from-the-heart thoughts on what you see as unique and
special about the birthday girl. Invite the other guests to do the
same. Then, before you cut the cake, each of you bless her by
showering her with words of affirmation and truth about who
she is and why you love her. (Unless it's chocolate cake. In that
case, by all means, cut the cake first; then bless her.)

Wambura

"Even the smallest wish-upon-a-star can expand
to Milky Way proportions when God gets a hold of it."
—PENNY, *SISTERCHICKS ON THE LOOSE!*

During my late teen years, I was convinced that the best—and probably only—way I could honor God with my life was by devoting myself to full-time ministry. The most noble of all mission fields was, of course, deepest, darkest Africa. I needed to go to Africa to serve God. That was all there was to it.

At a large missions conference, I filled out a form describing all my talents and skills. The form was then fed into a hulking computer, which matched my unique abilities with ministry openings around the world. I waited anxiously to receive the final printout of what I believed would be God's will for my life.

The answer came on a pale green and white striped scroll of computer paper that still had all the holes along both sides. In faded typed letters, my call to service read: "Laundry Supervisor, Nairobi, Kenya, East Africa."

What? Are you sure this is my printout? Oh, it is. Wow. Not what I'd expected.

Oh, sure, I believed a person could serve God in a beautiful way by washing clothes. It was just, well...I was hoping God's will for my future would be a little more...uh, spectacular. Yeah, that was it. More dramatic. I liked drama.

Then I realized that my list of qualifications, education, and abilities was rather limited. The "God's will" computer could only work with what it was given, and I could only work with what I was given, which was obviously not much.

I applied for the position with a humbled yet willing heart and excitedly told friends and family that I was going to leave soon to serve the Lord in Africa. They asked what I was going to do there. So I told them. "I'm going to supervise laundry."

All of them returned the same bemused, are-you-nuts sort of look. I took their responses as an opportunity to conjure up a more complete job description of how all the really important missionaries serving in that region must need someone dependable and energetic to organize their dirty clothes. I dramatized how I'd have to learn to walk down to the river with one of those tall baskets on my head and then pound out the African dirt with only a rock and my bare hands.

My friends and relatives were kind enough to withhold their comments on God's will for my life until the acceptance letter arrived. I waited weeks, months. Finally the envelope with the exotic stamp came.

"Dear Miss Jones. Greetings to you in the name of our Lord and Savior, Jesus Christ! We wish to thank you for applying...blah, blah,

blah...yet it is agreed that you lack sufficient experience and abilities for this position. May the Lord direct you to where you can best serve Him."

Crash and burn, baby! I never expected such a response. Apparently I was too ungifted and untalented to wash clothes for Jesus in Kenya. What, then, could I possibly do for Him?

At the time I was teaching a junior high girls' Sunday school class. All those impressionable young girls looked unblinkingly at me the next week when I told them I wasn't going to Africa after all. I would have to find something else I could do to serve the Lord in full-time ministry.

"You should tell stories," one of the girls suggested. Her name was Carolyn. She had gorgeous, thick, sun-kissed California hair and wore glasses. "We like the stories you tell us."

"Yes," said the other girls. "Your stories make us think about God in a new way."

I kept a rigid smile the rest of the morning for the girls' sake. Then I hurried home to cry alone in my room. I didn't think telling stories was a very nice suggestion from those girls! Telling stories had never solved problems for me. It had only started problems. I was reprimanded by a friend for "exaggerating the truth" about how much she wanted to get back together with her old boyfriend. I'd been punished at home more than once for "embellishing the truth." I'd been graded down on a science paper for "overstating the facts." (Hey, I just thought photosynthesis was a whole lot more interesting than the textbook made it out to be.)

Stories were not my friends. They betrayed me all the time. I thought in stories, dreamed in stories, wrote letters in stories. My imagination was always one ivy-covered glen ahead of me, egging me on.

No, stories couldn't possibly be my gift to humanity. I needed to do something tangible for the Lord. Something solid. Not something airy and capricious, like spinning fanciful tales.

I went to college, traveled in Europe, married a youth pastor, and had two babies. During that decade and a half, I continued to teach Sunday school and spend lots of time with teenage girls. In a concealed part of my spirit, I felt as if I had turned out to be a big disappointment. Yes, I was serving God with my husband in full-time ministry, but I wasn't like Carolyn, the young heart who first told me I should tell stories. She was now a missionary in Peru doing great work for God. She probably knew how to carry a basket on her head and everything.

Then, on a camping trip with our youth group, a tent full of thirteen-year-old girls challenged me to write the kind of stories they wanted to read. They even volunteered to help me by telling me everything I did wrong.

It took two years and weekly critique sessions with those teens before my first novel was published in what became the Christy Miller series. That book, *Summer Promise*, has been translated into five languages, and mail has come in from girls around the world saying that they gave their hearts to Christ after reading the story.

WIT 'N' WHIMSY

Q: What is the chief end of man?
A: Man's chief end is to glorify God and to enjoy him forever.
−FROM THE WESTMINSTER CATECHISM

"Love God, and do as you please."
−AUGUSTINE

One of the girls who read *Summer Promise* was Wambura. I met her at a writers' conference in England when we ended up at the same table for lunch. She spoke of the novel she was working on for young girls, a story to which girls in her culture would be able to relate.

Wambura's accent was British, but her skin and mannerisms reflected a more exotic homeland; so I had to ask her, "Wambura, where are you from? Where did you live when you read *Summer Promise*?"

"Nairobi, Kenya. It's in East Africa."

"Yes," I said, as an old familiar tha-thump quickened my heart. "I know exactly where Nairobi is. When I was your age, Wambura, I wanted to go there. I was going to supervise laundry."

She laughed with me.

"But I never went." My chin dipped with regret as I revealed the rest of the details. "I never made it to Kenya."

"Ah, but your story did come to Africa." Wambura's words were golden. "Perhaps you were never supposed to come. Only your stories. You sent your stories, and they have washed the hearts of many young girls just like me. In Nairobi and around the world. Do you see? God's will has been accomplished. You have been a supervisor of laundry."

Wambura now works for the International Bible Society. She's given me the privilege of mentoring her via e-mail as she writes her novel. One day I may actually go to Kenya. When I do, Wambura promises she'll put a basket on my head and watch me walk across the room. But we'll let her washing machine do our laundry.

*C*an you imagine how many grace-stories like Wambura's we will hear in heaven? Don't you love it when we hear some of them now?

Of course, we don't always get to see the rest of the story. And finding where we fit can be a big challenge at any age. Have you been rejected for some role you felt was God's plan for you? What was your response? How has God directed you since then?

Could it be that God had us in mind when He had the psalmist write, "He gives the rejects his hand, and leads them step-by-step" (Psalm 25:9)?

If you have seen God utilize the gifts and abilities He has given you, consider journaling about what He has done. Even if you are unable to share your grace-story verbally now, children and grandchildren and even nieces and nephews might enjoy reading your story someday.

Do you find yourself waiting for God to guide you to a new open door? God is always at work during the days of waiting. What new things are you learning, or what character traits is God developing in you?

If you wish the waiting process would go faster, get in line with the rest of us! God's perspective on timing is not the same as ours. Moses spent forty years as a shepherd before he was ready to lead God's people out of Egypt. Sarah waited decades to have a baby. And how many years did Jesus spend in the carpenter's shop? We are never breaking new ground when it comes to waiting for God's timing.

When God's directions do become clear, may each of us respond like Mary: "'I am the Lord's servant,' Mary answered. 'May it be to me as you [the angel who announced she would bear God's Son] have said'" (Luke 1:38, NIV).

In the meantime, let's agree to share our grace-stories here while we can and praise God at every opportunity. Then we'll be right on track when we gather together in heaven. What a fabulous celebration that will be. Can't wait!

But of course, waiting *is* our only option.

TAKE A CLOSER LOOK

- Genesis 37, 39–47:11. God meant it for good.
- Ephesians 5:19. Speak it, sing it!
- James 4:10. God will lift you up.

A Peep or Two from You

 Wisdom

"Everything comes from him;
Everything happens through him; Everything ends up in him.
Always glory! Always praise! Yes. Yes. Yes."

Romans 11:36

Quotable Sisterchicks

"God lets us fail in a secondary thing
that we may succeed in a primary."

Henrietta Mears

 Sisterchickin' Suggestion

Many women missionaries serve God in remote places.
Let them know that they are not forgotten! Put together a
surprise package for one of these Sisterchicks in the field.
You could include something fun to read, something new to wear,
fragrant lotion or a candle, a music CD, and a lovely sweet
of some sort that won't melt before it arrives.

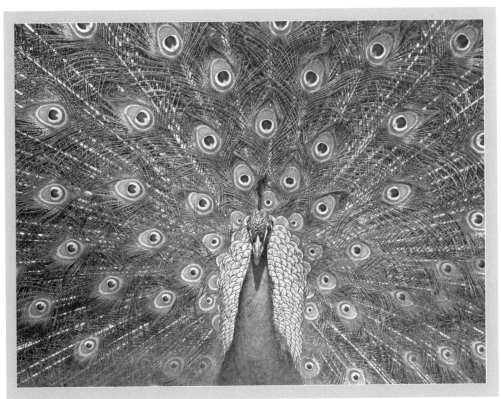

You think I'm gifted? Really? . . . I'm just not seeing it.

Under the Shadow of His Wing

*"He will cover you with his feathers,
and under his wings you will find refuge;
his faithfulness will be your shield and rampart."*

PSALM 91:4, NIV

*"Christ beside me, Christ before me,
Christ behind me, Christ within me,
Christ beneath me, Christ above me."*

SAINT PATRICK

Relentless Lover

FROM ROBIN'S NEST

"Do you suppose God enjoys us?
I know He loves us and provides for us,
but do you think He enjoys us as His artistic creation?"
—HOPE, *SISTERCHICKS DO THE HULA!*

How can you call yourself a Christian and write romance novels?"

That was the opening question tossed at me on a radio interview. We were on the air! Live! People were listening! And everyone, including me, was waiting to hear how I was going to answer.

A new but clear thought came to me in that moment. "Well, I think because when I was a teenager, I read a love story that changed my life."

"A love story?"

"Yes. In the first few chapters everything falls apart, and you think they are never going to get back together. About three-fourths of the way through, he does everything he can to prove his love to her, but still she won't come back. Then, in the last chapter, he comes riding in on a white horse and takes her to be with him forever."

The host looked at me skeptically. "How could a book like that change your life? It sounds like a formula romance novel to me."

"Really? A formula romance?"

"Yes. Isn't that what you were talking about?"

"Actually, I was talking about the Bible."

"The Bible?"

"Yes. There's a white horse and everything."

Suddenly that radio station experienced the dreaded dead air.

"We're going to cut to station break, but we'll be right back." The host pushed a few buttons and looked at me, stunned, before saying off the air, "You are absolutely right. I never saw that before. The Bible is the ultimate love story."

"God even calls us His bride," I added.

"You're right. He does."

Warming up to the idea, I went on to say that I thought God was the relentless Lover. He never stops pursuing us because we're His first love, and He wants us back.

When we returned to the air, the hour interview flew by with lively dialogue, as the host and I verbally contemplated God's love in a way that had us both speaking in thoughtful tones filled with awe.

In the weeks that followed, I thought a lot about what had happened during that interview. For hours I went through my Bible looking for places where God reveals His heart to us. How did I know we are His first love? Where does it say that? I wanted to be sure I hadn't made up anything.

Tiptoeing through the Old Testament, I became reacquainted with Jeremiah, Isaiah, and Joel. These books are laced with beautiful poetic phrases that pulsate with the heart cry of this relentless Lover.

- "Do not be afraid, for I have ransomed you. I have called you by name; you are mine" (Isaiah 43:1, NLT).
- "You are precious to me. You are honored, and I love you" (Isaiah 43:4, NLT).
- "But the Lord still waits for you to come to him so he can show you His love and compassion. For the Lord is a faithful God" (Isaiah 30:18, NLT).
- "Return to the Lord your God, for he is gracious and merciful. He is not easily angered. He is filled with kind-ness and is eager not to punish you.... And anyone who calls on the name of the Lord will be saved" (Joel 2:13, 32, NLT).

God's love letter to us is laced together with beautiful, soul-stirring evidence that we humans are indeed the object of His affection.

One of the verses I found brought a giddy sensation I recalled feeling way back in high school. I met a guy named Davey at a youth group event. As our church van was leaving the parking lot, Davey ran alongside, madly asking people for a pen so he could write down my phone number. A pen was tossed to him, and Davey wrote my name and number on his hand.

As I leaned out the open window and waved, he held up his hand and shouted, "See? I've got your number. I won't forget you!" All my girlfriends thought it was the most romantic gesture ever.

Davey called every night for a couple of weeks. But then the calls slowed and eventually stopped. I don't know what happened. Maybe he went to another youth group event and met another girl. Maybe he got busy and forgot all about me. But I never forgot how tender and thrilling it felt to watch someone come after me and write my name on his hand. That's why I love Isaiah 49:15–16: "I will not forget you. See, I have engraved you on the palms of my hands."

How sobering to know that instead of ink from a borrowed pen, the relentless Lover wrote our names on His hands with borrowed nails and His own blood.

After all these ages and all that has happened, we still remain the object of His affection. Amazing. Amazing grace.

WIT 'N' WHIMSY

"God loves each of us as if there were only one of us."

–AUGUSTINE

"Get into the habit of saying, 'Speak, Lord,' and life will become a romance."

–OSWALD CHAMBERS,
My Utmost for His Highest

*D*on't you just love a good romance? Every young couple thinks they are starring in one. Theirs is the greatest love story in history! They can't wait to be together, and they can't be together too much. In a group, they are like magnets, drawn to each other by an invisible force, helplessly, hopelessly in love.

Have you ever tried to describe how you feel when you know that God pursues you, loves you, wants to be with you, and wants to communicate with you?

Here's how one poet put it: "How precious it is, Lord, to realize that you are thinking about me constantly! I can't even count how many times a day your thoughts turn towards me. And when I waken in the morning, you are still thinking of me!" (Psalm 139:17–18, TLB). Talk about a magnetic attraction!

So what's up with the distraction that happens on our side of the relationship? How easily we forget that He is always with us.

What helps you to refocus on God during the day? Some savvy Sisterchicks gave these suggestions for remembering God's presence. Think of God:

- every time the phone rings.
- when the clock chimes.
- first thing in the morning before you get out of bed.
- every time you buckle up.

Have you ever written a letter to the Lord telling Him how you feel and what you think? What a tender gift that would be to Him.

When we know we are loved by God and that He is with us, we can face anything that comes our way with confidence. We also can live in joyful anticipation of what lies ahead: "Then I saw Heaven open wide—and oh! a white horse and its Rider. The Rider, named Faithful and True" (Revelation 19:11).

After that comes what we call "happily ever after"!

The Beginning.

Take a Closer Look

- Psalm 36:5–7. The measure of God's love.
- Psalm 42:8. A day-and-night kind of love.
- Psalm 139. Never-out-of-His-sight kind of love.

A Peep or Two from You

_____

_____

_____

_____

_____

_____

 WISDOM

"'I WANT THEM BACK, EVERY LAST ONE WHO BEARS MY NAME,

EVERY MAN, WOMAN, AND CHILD

WHOM I CREATED FOR MY GLORY,

YES, PERSONALLY FORMED AND MADE EACH ONE.'"

Isaiah 43:7

"YOUR BEAUTY AND LOVE CHASE AFTER ME

EVERY DAY OF MY LIFE.

I'M BACK HOME IN THE HOUSE OF GOD

FOR THE REST OF MY LIFE."

Psalm 23:6

January Madness

"Don't worry. Sometimes the 'January Madness'
lasts a little longer than usual."

—PENNY, *SISTERCHICKS ON THE LOOSE!*

In recognition of the "January Madness" that does indeed come upon me every year, I have instituted a traditional "Anti–January Madness" day during which I find my place. The procedure for this after-holiday special starts when I rise early, light a candle, make a pot of strong black tea, and set up camp in my favorite snuggle chair by the front window.

For hours I pour out my heart to God, writing page after page in a spiral-bound notebook. I consider a handful of difficult, deep thoughts that my soul has turned away during the frenetic schedule of the preceding months. I stare out the window and tell the trees that I feel just like them—stripped to the soul, with feeble arms upraised, waiting for spring to come again and cover me with the greenness of life and maybe a few pink frillies.

I love this January solitude, this day of anti-madness. I am empty, and the beautiful thing is, I know it! All I can do is sit there, rooted to the chair, fully dependent on Creator God for every leaf of life, every breath, every word. From this place of emptiness and expectation I wait, with my pot of tea, my pen and paper, and my ready heart.

Usually I start by writing out a long prayer. In this flowing conversation, dotted with lots of "wows!" and "thank-You-thank-You-thank-Yous!" I list significant moments from the past year. I tell God all over again how I think He is amazing and extravagant and patient. Sometimes I get kind of mushy, trying to find a way to tell Him how much I love Him. I also reflect on the painful moments and bow my spirit, ready to listen. Then I ask my Lord, "What's next?"

WIT 'N' WHIMSY

Looking for a proven way to minimize facial wrinkles, emotional overeating, and fatigue? Throw out those old, worn-out worries, and trust God. This system is free and available 24-7. Start your free trial with prayer now!

Sometimes I go back and read the journal pages from the prior year's day of Anti–January Madness. Every time I do, I am amazed at all that happened in one short year. I am even more amazed at how many catastrophes did *not* happen. I read lists of things I worried about and smile when I realize how few of those events happened. God provided. God healed. God blessed. God was there every single moment of that previous year. I can trust Him to be with me in the year ahead.

This past January, as I logged a summary of the prior year, I realized it had been a year of double blessings. Many of the same gifts were given to me twice in experiences and in people. I kept wondering why. *Why so much goodness from You last year, Lord?*

Silence. No explanation. No indication of what was expected of me in return for all the blessings. I was raised on the biblical premise that the one to whom much is given, much is required. So what was required of me?

My only lingering thought was, *Double portion, double portion. Who was the woman in Scripture who received the double portion?* It was Hannah. Every year she went with her husband to worship at Shiloh. First Samuel says, "But to Hannah he gave a double portion because he loved her" (1:5, NIV).

My heart did a little flutter when I read those words "because he loved her." Could it be that Hannah had received the double portion simply because she was loved—not because of anything she had done or not done? Is it that easy with God sometimes? Does He just bless us because He loves us?

I sat very still before the Lord and asked if that was it. *Did You bless me with a double portion last year just because You love me?*

The resounding echo in my spirit and in His Word was clearly yes! That was it. He loves us because He loves us. It is, sometimes, just that simple.

My day of contemplation ended differently than it had in years past. True, I scrawled lists of goals and anticipations for the coming year and recklessly spilled my heart onto the paper. (I also spilled a bit of tea on my snuggle chair!) But I didn't resurface with the usual heady sense of duty and a diagram of all the things I would accomplish for the King and for His kingdom in the coming year.

Instead, I took one steady step out of the cloud of January Madness and welcomed the year ahead feeling vibrantly alive. My spirit sprouted with the tender pinkness of anticipation for all that lay ahead in the new year.

With certainty I saw that when a woman knows she's loved, she can do anything. She can wait patiently for a slow promise to be fulfilled. She can withstand an impending storm. Such a woman does not merely grow older; she grows stronger in her sweet and abiding affection for the One who loves her.

*D*o you ever feel the need to stop the madness and find your place? That desire to refocus and push "reset" on our inner lives is a gift from God. It draws us away to time alone with Him. Jesus went alone into the hills. Robin has her snuggle chair. Susanna Wesley, mother of nineteen children, would throw her apron up over her head when she needed a moment to herself.

How about you? Where do you go when you meet with Jesus?

Want to know what other Sisterchicks do when they set aside time to spend with the Lord?

- Determined Sisterchicks have been known to turn off the ringers on the phones or to let their servants, the answering machine, take their calls. After all, they are in an important meeting, for heaven's sake, and can't possibly be disturbed!
- Romantic Sisterchicks light a candle, even in the daytime.
- Musical Sisterchicks listen to or sing worship songs.
- Bored Sisterchicks read a new translation or paraphrase of the Bible.
- Creative Sisterchicks might sing or dance before the Lord.
- Nature-loving Sisterchicks take a walk.

You get the idea. We have the freedom to make this time special in our own way. Regardless of where or how we spend time with God, the stunning truth is ever before us: God loves us because He wants to. No other reason. We don't deserve it, and we can't earn it. All we can do is choose to believe it.

Some classic elements for a quiet time include:

- Remember with prayer and thanksgiving what God has done in the past.
- Lay out all your questions before the Lord.
- Listen for what He has to say as you pray and read His words.

Keep an eye out for evidence of God's everlasting love for you today. It's like a giant Easter egg hunt! Proof of His love is lying around everywhere. Carry a big basket, and fill it up.

TAKE A CLOSER LOOK

- 1 Chronicles 16:12. Remember!
- Psalm 62:5. Rest for the soul.
- Matthew 4:4. Better than bread.

A Peep or Two from You

_____

_____

_____

_____

_____

_____

_____

_____

_____

_____

 WISDOM

"'HERE'S WHAT I WANT YOU TO DO: FIND A QUIET, SECLUDED PLACE

SO YOU WON'T BE TEMPTED TO ROLE-PLAY BEFORE GOD.

JUST BE THERE AS SIMPLY AND HONESTLY AS YOU CAN MANAGE.

THE FOCUS WILL SHIFT FROM YOU TO GOD, AND YOU

WILL BEGIN TO SENSE HIS GRACE.'"

Matthew 6:6

"'GIVE YOUR ENTIRE ATTENTION TO WHAT GOD IS DOING RIGHT NOW,
AND DON'T GET WORKED UP ABOUT WHAT MAY OR
MAY NOT HAPPEN TOMORROW. GOD WILL HELP YOU DEAL
WITH WHATEVER HARD THINGS COME UP WHEN THE TIME COMES.'"

Matthew 6:34

QUOTABLE SISTERCHICKS

"Worry does not empty tomorrow of its sorrow;
it empties today of its strength."

CORRIE TEN BOOM

"For we are so preciously loved by God that we
cannot even comprehend it. No created being can
ever know how much and how sweetly and
tenderly God loves them. It is only with the help of
his grace that we are able to persevere in spiritual
contemplation with endless wonder at his high,
surpassing, immeasurable love
which our Lord in his goodness has for us."

JULIAN OF NORWICH

God Planted a Garden

FROM ROBIN'S NEST

*"The sweetness of that fragrant moment lingered.
I held in my breath, as if I had somehow caught a rare whiff
of all that is eternal."*

—HOPE, *SISTERCHICKS DO THE HULA!*

Determined to brighten up the view outside my front window, I bought a flat of primroses last week. The stretch of stormy weather we had been experiencing made the purchase a bold gesture and might even have been considered an act of faith.

However, this morning, with a dramatic ta-da! the sun returned, giving no apology for its long absence. I bounced out the front door while the day was still fresh and new. I couldn't wait to sink my hands into the steamy earth. Oh, the unforgettable smell of fresh soil! Don't you love it when the earth is pliable in your hands?

As I dug into my small garden, I wondered how Creator God must have felt when He planted His garden in Eden. How did it smell? How did the earth feel in His hands? What did He see in the unformed clay?

For the first five days of creation, God merely spoke, "and it was so." At His command, solar systems lined up and spun in perfect harmony. Sheltering oaks stretched toward the sky, spreading their limbs, needing only a word to make them comply.

Did God whisper the first snowflake into the air? Did He bellow a word that incited mountains to rise out of nothing? Did He speak with a smile when He told the hummingbirds to "be"? Did one long roll of His laughing words spill daffodils across a meadow? So much to wonder about.

All He tells us is that He spoke, "and it was so."

Yet when God made the first human, He did more than just speak. He touched.

Creator God reached into the fresh, steamy earth and crafted the first human with His own hands. He didn't hesitate to get His hands dirty to bring us to Himself. Did it feel good to Him when we were but dust and still so pliable in His grip? Did He go home at the end of that day with us still under His fingernails?

Kneeling in my small patch of earth, I felt enlivened by the mystery of it all. God planted a garden. He scooped up His earth and handcrafted Adam and Eve. Then He spoke. He said His work was "very good." Did Adam and Eve realize that truth when God walked with them in the garden in the cool of the evening?

We know that a woman listened to a smooth lie in that garden. She did not walk away. She did not repeat the truth she had been told by God. She listened to the lie and believed it.

I have been that woman. I know how convincing the facts can sound when they are bent just right. Like Eve, I also know the heaviness of shame that pushes me away from God and into hiding. I, too, have heard His voice when He calls to me as He did to Adam and Eve, "Where are you?"

This question echoes in the garden of every heart as clearly now as it did the first time God spoke it. "Where are you?" The relentless Lover still seeks His own because we are His first love, and He wants us back.

Almighty God could have been done with us and this broken planet long, long ago. Yet the mystery grew. The mercy expanded.

In the garden, in the seeds, in the seasons, and in the earth itself, there still lingers an occasional rare whiff of all that is eternal. We see it every spring when that which appeared dead sprouts with new life. I saw it that morning while planting the primroses. Even the soil that was cursed so long ago still miraculously nurtures and yields rich blessings. We have not been forgotten by the One who made us.

God stood one morning in another garden, a garden where a stone was rolled away from a tomb. What Creator God did at that garden tomb in the rising warmth of the early morning was very, very good. A promise He had made in the first garden was at last fulfilled. Truth had crushed the lie. Life had swallowed death.

There is another woman in this second garden. She lingered in front of the open tomb and asked what must have sounded to God like the echo of His heart at long last returning to Him on the lips of His creation. She asked, "Where is He?" Now she was the one who wanted Him back.

As she turned and looked through tear-rimmed eyes at the resurrected Savior, she thought He was the gardener. Could it be that His spike-scarred hands still carried evidence of Eden's soil beneath His fingernails?

*A*s it was in the beginning, so it is even to this day! God is still getting His hands in the dirt as He carefully tends our earthbound lives. Listen in on this prayer from one of His girls:

> *Waiting on You, Lord, I am restless. Not quieted and*
> *serene. The garden of my heart is not a place of beauty*
> *and calm. It is stacked with broken twigs, thorny bushes,*
> *and rows of brambles. Life does not happen here. Only*
> *reordering of the broken bits. Great Gardener of my soul,*
> *enter the gate too long shut to You. Bring Your tools.*
> *Clean away all that does not produce sweet fruit that is*
> *pleasing to You. Remove all the broken bits. Work the*
> *ground. Clear the paths. Bring life. So that all who stop for*
> *a visit may find rest and refreshment for their souls.*
> *(From Robin's journal)*

Sometimes all we have to bring to the Gardener of our souls is broken bits. Amazingly, He gathers up the pain, sorrow, and sin. Then He heals, restores, and forgives.

Does your soul's landscape need pruning and restoring? The Gardener is open for business. Bring what is in your garden to Him now, and lay it all out. Ask Him to spruce things up and bring order back.

Here's what Jesus' brother James says to do when we come to the Lord all wild and weedy. "So throw all spoiled virtue and cancerous evil in the garbage. In simple humility, let our gardener, God, landscape you with the Word, making a salvation-garden of your life" (James 1:21).

Has God been landscaping you with the Word lately?

Just like earthly gardeners, when the hard work is done, God delights in His handiwork. "Walk into the fields and look at the wildflowers. They don't fuss with their appearance—but have you ever seen color and design quite like it? The ten best-dressed men and women in the country look shabby alongside them. If God gives such attention to the wildflowers, most of them never even seen, don't you think he'll attend to you, take pride in you, do his best for you?" (Luke 12:27–28)

How has God been "attending" to you? How do you feel about His taking pride in you? How have you noticed Him doing His best for you?

Since God is the Gardener of our lives, maybe we're Sisterchicks *and* flower girls!

WIT 'N' WHIMSY

Is life "stinky" right now? You know, plants do grow best with a good dose of fertilizer.

The same God who created roses, clouds, and butterflies also made cockroaches. What was He thinking?

"For my thoughts are not your thoughts, neither are your ways my ways." (Isaiah 55:8, NIV)

Take a Closer Look

- Psalm 33:13–15. The view from where God sits.
- John 15:1–17. Jesus is the vine, which makes us the what?
- Isaiah 58:11. The cure for sun-scorched plants.

A Peep or Two from You

_____

_____

_____

_____

 WISDOM

"THERE HAS NEVER BEEN THE SLIGHTEST DOUBT IN MY MIND

THAT THE GOD WHO STARTED THIS GREAT WORK IN YOU

WOULD KEEP AT IT AND BRING IT TO A FLOURISHING FINISH

ON THE VERY DAY CHRIST JESUS APPEARS."

Philippians 1:6

"MAKE SURE NO ONE GETS LEFT OUT OF GOD'S GENEROSITY.

KEEP A SHARP EYE OUT FOR WEEDS OF BITTER DISCONTENT.

A THISTLE OR TWO GONE TO SEED CAN RUIN

A WHOLE GARDEN IN NO TIME."

Hebrews 12:15

QUOTABLE SISTERCHICKS

"What sort of world might it have been if Eve had refused the Serpent's offer and had said to him instead, 'Let me not be like God. Let me be what I was made to be—let me be a woman.'"

ELISABETH ELLIOT

Stars Were Singing

FROM ROBIN'S NEST

"The stars were singing. I know they were."
—HOPE, *SISTERCHICKS DO THE HULA!*

In the church of my childhood, if you found the kids volunteering for nursery duty or up in the balcony on a Sunday evening passing notes, you knew a missionary was in town. While my contemporaries scattered on those Sunday nights, I took a seat in the front row—the undisputed nerd locale. I was captivated by firsthand accounts of faraway places where skinny people wore bones in their noses and danced around a fire with spears in their hands. I couldn't get enough of the missionary slide shows and always felt sad when the inevitable sunset picture appeared on the screen.

What I loved most was watching the guest missionaries' faces as they talked about "their" people, the indigenous groups they lived with in remote villages. I could always tell which missionaries truly loved their people. Their voices would soften, and their eyes would sparkle as they told their stories.

I wanted to be like them. All the heroines of my youth were missionary women. I thought that to love like that and to give your life to an unreached people was one of the most genuine acts of human compassion.

One soothing Southern California evening, we had a guest missionary speaker who topped them all. He had sought after and entered a region where a primal, stripped-down society was living the same way their ancestors had for hundreds of years. No Westerner had ever entered the remote region. No traces of modern civilization had come their way.

When the missionary at long last acquired enough understanding of their language, he told them about God's Son, who had come to this earth and made a way for us to be reunited with our heavenly Father.

Eyes of the villagers lit up with recognition. "Yes! What is His name?"

"Jesus Christ."

Great delight spread among the villagers as they repeated the blessed name and pointed to the stars overhead.

"We know His story," they said. "He was sent by God, born of a virgin, killed without doing wrong, and He came back to life."

"Yes!" the missionary said excitedly. "But how did you know all this?"

"The stars. Do you not see the story? It is all there. Written in the heavens. Our ancients told us. They knew God had a Son. But they never knew His name. We have waited all this time for you to come so we might learn his name. Jesus."

How did God do that? How did He put the truth in their hearts? How did they know to connect the dots of the stars in a way that showed them pictures of eternity?

The marvel and the mystery of this great celestial show still draws me to the front row every time God dims the lights and starts His slide show in the night sky. Could this be the real reason the stars twinkle? God is telling His story to us, His unreached people. And whenever the One who truly loves lost people speaks of them, His voice softens and His eyes sparkle. Just like stars.

*I*magine how awestruck that missionary must have felt when he heard the truth of these verses from those isolated villagers:

> "The heavens declare the glory of God;
> the skies proclaim the work of his hands.
> Day after day they pour forth speech;
> night after night they display knowledge.
> There is no speech or language
> where their voice is not heard.
> Their voice goes out into all the earth,
> their words to the ends of the world." (Psalm 19:1–4, NIV)

God has set eternity in the hearts of all humanity, and He has made a way for all of us to hear His story. In what ways did God prepare your heart to hear His story? Trace God's footprints as He made Himself known to you. What amazes you the most about your spiritual journey?

It's astounding that God wants to use us to spread the Good News of His only Son, Jesus. As we share life with the people God places around us, maybe we'll get to hear echoes of God's preparation in their hearts. Imagine how awestruck we'll be!

TAKE A CLOSER LOOK

- Ecclesiastes 3:11. Eternity in our hearts.
- Isaiah 40:26. Naming stars.
- 1 Corinthians 3:6–9. God's coworkers.

A Peep or Two from You

_____

_____

_____

_____

_____

_____

_____

_____

_____

_____

_____

_____

_____

_____

WISDOM

"WHEN I CONSIDER YOUR HEAVENS,

THE WORK OF YOUR FINGERS,

THE MOON AND THE STARS,

WHICH YOU HAVE SET IN PLACE,

WHAT IS MAN THAT YOU ARE MINDFUL OF HIM,

THE SON OF MAN THAT YOU CARE FOR HIM?

YOU MADE HIM A LITTLE LOWER THAN THE HEAVENLY BEINGS

AND CROWNED HIM WITH GLORY AND HONOR....

O LORD, OUR LORD,

HOW MAJESTIC IS YOUR NAME IN ALL THE EARTH!"

Psalm 8:3 — 5, 9, NIV

"That there is a God my Reason would soon tell me by the wondrous workes that I see, the vast frame of the Heaven and the Earth, the order of all things, night and day, Summer and Winter, Spring and Autumne, the dayly providing for this great household upon the Earth, the preserving and directing of All to its proper end."

ANNE BRADSTREET

 SISTERCHICKIN' SUGGESTION

Why not host a Sisterchicks Night Out Under the Stars? Grab a few friends, and get away from the city lights. Pack a basket with a thermos, some brownies, your Bible, and a flashlight. The flashlight will come in handy as you read Psalm 19 aloud while taking in the night sky's lessons. Nothing compares to sitting under the immense canopy of space and sensing truth that was invisible to you in the bright and busy midday. Pass around your reflections on the wonders of God along with the brownies and coffee.

A G R A C E   N O T E

---

*F*arewell, dear Sisterchicks! Cindy and I have loved sharing our hearts with you. Oh, the grace-stories of your life that have not yet been written! Always remember that the cage's latch was lifted for all of us when the stone was rolled away. You are His, and you are deeply loved.

> "Now God has us where he wants us, with all the time in
> this world and the next to shower grace and kindness
> upon us in Christ Jesus." (Ephesians 2:7)

So come closer. No, closer. Right up to the edge. A better thing this grace now brings. It bids you fly and gives you wings! Ready? On the count of three.

One

Two

Three

TAKE FLIGHT!

I'll Fly Away

EXERPT FROM THE SONG BY
ALBERT E. BRUMLEY

Some glad morning

When this life is o'er

I'll fly away;

To a home on God's celestial shore,

I'll fly away.

PHOTO: JOHN HANNAH

Oh, glory!

ACKNOWLEDGMENTS

*O*ur fine feathered friends, who gave us so much encouragement on this book, thank you.

Carrie, our faithful prayer pal, along with Kim, Elaine, and Shelly. Paula, our favorite worship troubadour, who propped up our spirits while monitoring our progress. Anne, who loves deeply and fed us courage in e-mails sent from across the glimmering sea. Karen, our generous writer comrade, who gave us the key to her getaway cabin so we could create uninterrupted. Ross and Rachel, who have spent their lives quietly blushing while their mom tells stories about them. The elders' wives from New Heights Church, who offered feedback on the first draft. Ben and Amy Hannan, who have schooled their mother in grace and patience and asked her more questions than everyone else put together. Jim and Rhea Turner, who always believed their daughter, Cindy, should write a book. Janet and Julee, our editors extraordinaire, along with the Multnomah publishing team: Sharon, Angela, and Kevin.

And forever and for always, our husbands. Robin loves Ross. Cindy loves Matt. And that's that.

All of you guys were—we just have to say this—the wind beneath our wings. (Okay, that's our final bird yolk, we mean joke.)

Watch for the next

Sisterchick devotional

coming in fall 2007!

SISTERCHICK® Adventures by
ROBIN JONES GUNN

SISTERCHICKS ON THE LOOSE!

Zany antics abound when best friends Sharon and Penny take off on a midlife adventure to Finland, returning home with a new view of God and a new zest for life.

SISTERCHICKS DO THE HULA!

It'll take more than an unexpected stowaway to keep two middle-aged sisterchicks from reliving their college years with a little Waikiki wackiness—and learning to hula for the first time.

SISTERCHICKS IN SOMBREROS!

Two Canadian sisters embark on a journey to claim their inheritance—beachfront property in Mexico—not expecting so many bizarre, wacky problems! But there's nothing a little coconut cake can't cure...

AVAILABLE NOW!

www.sisterchicks.com

More SISTERCHICK® Adventures by
ROBIN JONES GUNN

SISTERCHICKS DOWN UNDER!

Kathleen meets Jill at the Chocolate Fish café in New Zealand, and they instantly forge a friendship. Together they fall head over heels into a deeper sense of God's love.

SISTERCHICKS SAY OOH LA LA!

Painting toenails and making promises under the canopy of a princess bed seals a friendship for life! Fifty years of ups and downs find Lisa and Amy still Best Friends Forever…and off on an unforgettable Paris rendezvous!

SISTERCHICKS IN GONDOLAS

At a fifteenth-century palace in Venice, best friends/sisters-in-law Jenna and Sue welcome the gondola-paced Italian lifestyle! And over boiling pots of pasta, they dare each other to dream again.

AVAILABLE NOW!

www.sisterchicks.com

More Titles from Robin Jones Gunn

TEA AT GLENBROOKE

Snuggle into an overstuffed chair, sip your favorite tea, and journey to Glenbrooke… "a quiet place where souls are refreshed." Written from a tender heart, Robin Jones Gunn transports you to an elegant place of respite, comfort, and serenity—a place you'll never want to leave! Lavishly illustrated by Susan Mink Colclough, look forward to a joyful reading experience that captures the essence of a peaceful place.

ISBN 1-58860-023-8

MOTHERING BY HEART

Focusing upon the special bond between a mother and child, this unique gift book offers lilting poetry, poignant prose, spiritual insights, romantic photographic images, inspiring quotations, and heart-warming journal entries. A delightful companion to women of every age and background celebrating the vast and myriad joys of motherhood!

ISBN 1-57673-914-7

GENTLE PASSAGES

As she shares her own special traditions, Robin Jones Gunn makes the passage into womanhood a tender and joyful celebration—an invitation to a treasured role in God's eyes.

ISBN 1-57673-943

Come to Glenbrooke...
"A Quiet Place Where Souls Are Refreshed."

The Glenbrooke Series